MW00358372

COLLEGE IS NOT FOR EVERYONE

Louis Rosen

ScarecrowEducation
Lanham, Maryland • Toronto • Oxford
2005

Published in the United States of America
by ScarecrowEducation
An imprint of The Rowman & Littlefield Publishing Group, Inc.
4501 Forbes Boulevard, Suite 200, Lanham, Maryland 20706
www.scarecroweducation.com

PO Box 317
Oxford
OX2 9RU, UK

Copyright © 2005 by Louis Rosen

All rights reserved. No part of this publication may be reproduced, stored
in a retrieval system, or transmitted in any form or by any means, electronic,
mechanical, photocopying, recording, or otherwise, without the prior permission
of the publisher.

British Library Cataloguing in Publication Information Available

Library of Congress Cataloging-in-Publication Data

Rosen, Louis, Ph. D.
  College is not for everyone / Louis Rosen.
    p. cm.
  Includes bibliographical references and index.
  ISBN 1-57886-245-0 (pbk. : alk. paper)
  1. College attendance—United States. 2. Education, Higher—Standards—
United States. 3. Vocational guidance—United States. I. Title.

LC148.2.R67 2005
378.1'694—dc22

                                                        2004029878

♾™ The paper used in this publication meets the minimum requirements of
American National Standard for Information Sciences—Permanence of Paper
for Printed Library Materials, ANSI/NISO Z39.48-1992.
Manufactured in the United States of America.

CONTENTS

FIGURES

TABLES

INTRODUCTION

There is certainly nothing wrong with going to college. Colleges and universities prepare the highly skilled professionals in our society. Highly trained doctors, nurses, engineers, lawyers, scientists, business professionals, and teachers are part of what has made America the most prosperous and healthiest nation the world has ever known. But carpenters, secretaries, machinists, farmworkers, and salespersons are important to our nation as well. We need to be careful not to be guilty of devaluing those students who choose not to go to college. Not everyone wants or needs a college education. That statement is heresy to many of the most important people making decisions about the direction of education in the United States.

It is time to take another look at our priorities for education. Priorities based on elitism rather than what our youth want and need to prepare them for realities in the marketplace are not serving our nation well. The current emphasis on academics is providing a direction that is painfully wrong for at least a third of students now attending our nation's schools. We need to have the same kind of passion for those who decide that they do not want or need a college education as we do for those who decide to pursue an education beyond high school. It is time to treat all of our youth equally.

The trend for higher academic standards for education has now been in existence for over a decade. Politicians claim that they are working. Educators and employers are not so sure. The current No Child Left Behind Act attempts to track high academic standards in reading, math, and science subject areas in grades 3–8 and attempts to tie federal funding to progress. By 2005, schools must assess each student once in grades 10–12 in math and reading. Although all schools in a state must report test results, only schools receiving Title I funds that fail for two consecutive years to make "average yearly progress" (AYP) will receive sanctions. Nationally, 95 percent of school districts get Title I funds. Initially there was bipartisan support for the No Child Left Behind Act and state legislators and educational policy makers were in favor of higher standards and evaluation. At present, many state legislatures and school districts are saying the money is not as significant as promised and the requirements of the legislation endanger local and state control over education.

While states and large school districts may be split over support for No Child Left Behind Act (American Federation of Teachers 2004), state legislatures have increasingly taken up the banner to increase graduation requirements. Twenty states have now implemented graduate exit examinations as of August 2004. In many cases, those exit examinations include test items on algebra and geometry as well as higher reading scores. In inner-city and in many rural schools, students are having difficulty passing graduate exit examinations. The Educational Policy Commission Study for 2003 (Gayler et al. 2003) indicates that there is positive evidence that the exit exams are increasing the drop-out rate in several states where they are administered. There are serious questions being asked by many state education policy makers related to whether exit exams are being used as a filter system rather than "raising the bar" of expectations. In many cases, exit exams may be increasing the drop-out rate; at the very least, they discourage students from attending school on a regular basis.

Graduate exit examinations and the demand for higher academic standards posed by the No Child Left Behind Act are raising some serious questions for many states and school boards. Some of those questions are:

- Are the higher expectations in reading, math, and science appropriate for all students?

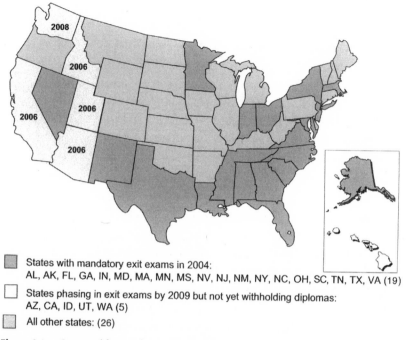

States with mandatory exit exams in 2004:
AL, AK, FL, GA, IN, MD, MA, MN, MS, NV, NJ, NM, NY, NC, OH, SC, TN, TX, VA (19)

States phasing in exit exams by 2009 but not yet withholding diplomas:
AZ, CA, ID, UT, WA (5)

All other states: (26)

Figure I.1. States with Mandatory Exit Exams
Source: Center on Education Policy, based on information collected from the State Department of Education, July 2004

- Is the current emphasis on all students being prepared to go on to college realistic in terms of the aspirations of many high school graduates to go to work directly out of high school?
- Will the advocates of "every child a college education" dilute the purpose of the university system due to too many students and insufficient funding?
- Are the new requirements of the No Child Left Behind Act and exit examinations helping or hurting the aspirations and goals of many of our students and therefore causing an increase in the drop-out rate?
- Is the emphasis on higher verbal and math scores realistic with current and projected demands of the workplace?
- Is the public ready to give up on the benefits of the comprehensive public high school?
- Will funding for the No Child Left Behind Act deplete the resources for vocational education programs?

- Exactly where are the jobs today and how much preparation is needed to fill those jobs?
- Can education realistically be blamed for economic problems of the United States?
- Will the current emphasis on college for everyone make our high schools glorified college-prep schools?
- Is the current emphasis on college for everyone really hiding an "educate the best and shoot the rest" philosophy?

These are only some of the questions this book attempts to answer. Every teacher, parent, school administrator, school board member, and legislator obviously needs to come to his or her own conclusions but this book hopes to provide some factual information and perspective that may be helpful. We all know that education is expensive, both in money and in time spent. The lives of our children and youth are too important to let politicians alone provide the answers to some of these very important questions. We must be careful not to sell out local control in order to meet school district and state budgets. If it is true that all politics is local, then education—which is about as local as you can get—needs policies that are set by local school board members, not legislators and politicians in Washington. Wrong answers to the questions posed above will lead local educators in a misguided direction that will take years to correct. Hopefully, some of the factual information used in this book will help us head in the right direction in terms of providing real equality and educational opportunity for all of our children.

1

EXACTLY WHERE ARE MOST OF THE JOBS TODAY?

There are many educational policy makers and politicians who believe that education is necessary if youths are to have a job and if the United States is to maintain its superiority as a world economic power. We need to take a look at where the jobs are today and make some conclusions as to whether the educational policy makers and politicians are correct in terms of whether a college education is necessary in order to have one of those jobs.

All you need to do is purchase or check out from your local library *World Almanac and Book of Facts* (2005) and turn to the statistics listed under employment or jobs. This will give you an impartial listing of the job categories used by the Bureau of Labor Statistics to classify the number of jobs in various job categories. You may be surprised by what you find. A list of jobs can easily be divided into jobs that do not require a college degree and jobs that need some further training beyond high school. A suggested list of job classifications used by the Bureau of Labor Statistics that do not require a college education has been compiled in table 1.1.

Another resource that is available in your local library in order to come to some conclusions about jobs that do not require a college education is the *Occupational Outlook Handbook* (U.S. Department of Labor 2001). The *Handbook* is used by employment counselors throughout the nation to provide

Table 1.1. Jobs Not Requiring a College Degree in 2003 (Same Technical Training Recommended in Most Cases)

Healthcare Support Occupations	2,926,000
Protective Service Occupations	2,727,000
Food Preparation and Serving-Related Occupations	7,254,000
Building, Groundskeeping, and Maintenance	4,947,000
Personal Care and Service Occupations	4,232,000
Sales and Sales-Related Occupations	15,960,000
Office and Administrative Support Occupations	19,536,000
Farming, Fishing, and Forestry Occupations	1,050,000
Construction and Extraction Occupations	8,114,000
Installation, Maintenance, and Repair Occupations	5,041,000
Production Occupations	9,700,000
Transportation and Material-Moving Occupations	8,320,000
Total Number of Noncollege Jobs	89,807,000

Source: *World Almanac Book of Facts,* 2005.

information about various jobs to prospective employees. Jobs that the *Occupational Outlook Handbook* describes as not needing any further training beyond high school include roofers, plasterers, stucco masons, insulation workers, painters, glaziers, grocery clerks, butchers, elevator installers, assemblers, blue-collar supervisors, goods processors, waiters and waitresses, forestry and logging workers, printers, woodworkers, taxi drivers, many sales occupations, bakers, highway services and construction workers, and farmworkers.

Jobs listed in the *Occupational Outlook Handbook* as needing some training or a certificate or license prior to application but not necessarily a college education are insurance adjuster and underwriting, court reporter, computer software programmer, earthmoving equipment operator, travel agent, dental assistant, home health aide, child care worker, airframe mechanic, airplane power plant mechanic, automotive repair technician, heating and air conditioning mechanic, nurse's aide, millwright, electrician, plumber, sheet metal worker, long-distance truck driver, police officer, and firefighter.

It is important to note that none of the jobs listed above requires a four-year college education. It is also important to note that some of the training for many of these jobs has traditionally come from the community college. There is concern that community colleges have had to cut many job preparation programs in order to make room for more courses that prepare students for four-year colleges.

Table 1.2.   Jobs Requiring a College or Graduate Degree in 2003

Management, Business, and Financial Operations	19,934,000
Management Occupations	14,468,000
Business and Financial Operations	5,465,000
Computer and Mathematical Occupations	3,122,000
Architecture and Engineering Occupations	2,727,000
Life, Physical, and Social Science Occupations	1,375,000
Community and Social Services Occupations	2,184,000
Legal Occupations	1,508,000
Education, Training, and Library Occupations	7,768,000
Arts, Design, Entertainment, Sports and Media Occupations	2,663,000
Healthcare Practitioner and Technical Occupations	6,648,000
Total Number of Jobs Needing a College Education	67,862,000

Source: *World Almanac Book of Facts*, 2005

Another list can be compiled that tells us the categories of jobs listed by the Bureau of Labor Statistics as needing a four-year college degree or graduate work. That list is shown in table 1.2.

What do the numbers tell us?

A quick assessment of the figures listed by Bureau of Labor Statistics (U.S. Department of Labor 1989) leads us to the conclusion that more than half the jobs in the United States today do not require a college degree. Many of the advocates of the "College for Everyone" philosophy seem to be telling us that if you do not go to college you are doomed to a life of unemployment and poverty. This is simply not true. That does not mean that a college degree or at least some college or technical training is not desirable or would not lead to a much higher income over a lifetime. Statistics indicate that the more schooling you have, the higher your standard of living—in most cases. The U.S. Department of Education, National Center for Education Statistics (NCES 1997), provides us with a graph that demonstrates how education correlates directly to projected income (see figure 1.1).

While there seems little doubt that more education may lead to a richer lifestyle economically, there may be some doubt in assuming that money is a key to happiness. There are many lawyers, doctors, dentists, business executives, and engineers who hate their jobs. There are also many secretaries, carpenters, taxi drivers, and gardeners who love what they do and would not trade it for a high-paying job. We need to be careful and not make

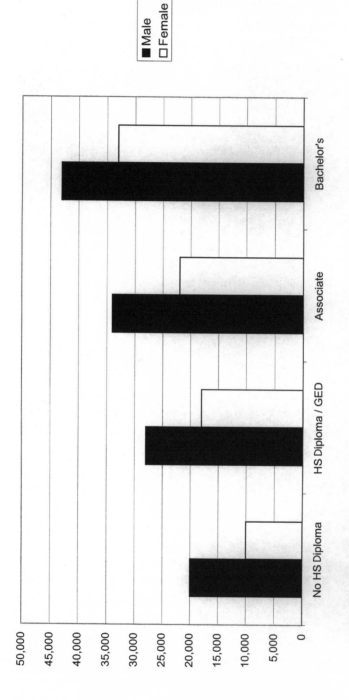

Office of Vocational and Adult Education, U.S. Department of Education, 2003

Figure 1.1. Potential Earnings by Education Level Completed

value judgments that earning a great deal of money means the same thing to all people. Obviously, some people would rather have a simple job, without stress and without aggravation, than a high-paying job full of ulcers and heart attacks. Choosing an occupation should be more about liking the tasks involved in the job than money. Wise parents and job counselors already know this.

EMPLOYMENT, UNEMPLOYMENT, AND THE ECONOMY

There is continual concern about the unemployment rate in the United States, which in 2003 and 2004 ran between 5 and 6 percent. The nation lost 2.3 million jobs from 2001 until the end of 2003 when a mild recovery began. Job creation has been weaker than in any economic recovery since 1945. Job creation picked up slowly toward the end of 2003 and in the beginning months of 2004, but the jobs were mostly in lower-wage positions (Committee on Education and the Workforce 2004). Many job seekers have given up looking for work, thereby further confusing statistics about the rate of unemployment. The high cost of health benefits has been said to limit the number of jobs offered by businesses to potential employees, thus creating more part-time and low-paying jobs. There is also continual concern about job outsourcing or the movement of manufacturing to other nations because of cheap labor—as well as the need to bring in foreign workers because there is a shortage of American workers to fill certain types of skilled labor positions (Chen and Hayasaki 2004). Unemployment statistics generally play a key role in presidential campaigns. The reality is that a correlation between who is president and either high or low employment is highly suspect. Employment may be more dependent on technological advancements, the balance of trade, immigration, and economic cycles rather than who is president of the United States. The president can, however, use the office of the presidency as a bully pulpit to lead education in the right direction in terms of job preparation. Too often, politicians pay no attention to the facts but rely instead on what they think a certain segment of the public wants to hear. College for everyone may be what some segments of the public want to hear but there are other segments that would more favorably respond to realistic job preparation for their children and grandchildren.

In a recent interview, Alan Greenspan, president of the Federal Reserve Board, said that improved education was the best long-term solution to the job losses caused by globalization and other economic gyrations (Committee on Education and the Workforce 2004). But what kind of education was Greenspan talking about? Was he talking about more college-trained liberal arts majors or more engineers? There are 1.3 million young people graduating from college this year. Most of those young people are without jobs. Was Greenspan talking about more journeyman electricians or more pre-law students? Improved education means different things to different people.

Over the past thirty years, job training policies and programs have focused on the "supply side" of the training equation. The "demand" side has often been overlooked. Too often, emphasis on the supply side is disappointing to youth when they discover there is no need for the training they received in either college or trade school. There needs to be a close watch in terms of what jobs are actually out there in order to cut the time lag between training and employment. (Chapter 8 describes some of the occupational needs and job preparation in greater detail.)

In 2002, $1.28 billion was awarded overall to the Carl D. Perkins Vocational and Applied Technology Act. This act is to provide funds for schools, school districts, and community agencies to facilitate training and placement in the workforce. The act was up for reauthorization in 2004. The question for the federal government and the administrators of the Carl D. Perkins Act is, will the act be a way in which the federal government can help local education agencies create or reinstate vocational education programs in schools or will the act be another ploy to attract students with high academic skills to college preparatory programs in technical areas?

EDUCATION AND THE ECONOMY: ARE OUR SCHOOLS FAILING US?

During the *A Nation at Risk* scare of the early 1990s, critics accused educators of failing to prepare workers for the challenge of the marketplace. As growth in U.S. productivity slowed during the 1980s and 1990s, other countries achieved productivity levels similar to those in the United States. Competition for markets for U.S. businesses increased. Some attributed the loss of markets to the limited ability of the U.S. educational system to provide students with skills necessary to succeed in today's labor market.

The reality is that other factors, not education, were the reason for the closing of the trade gap. Capital investment, technical innovation, foreign trade, and government regulation played much larger roles in slowing down productivity than the educational system. Worker productivity is measured by output per worker or per hour worked. Many things, including the skills of the workforce, affect worker productivity. Worker productivity has grown almost continuously since the end of World War II, rising to a level in 1994 that is approximately three times that of 1947 (U.S. Department of Labor 1992). (See figure 1.2.)

It is true that other nations are catching up with U.S. worker productivity. That is due to a number of factors, including recovering from WWII, shifts toward free enterprise and away from a managed economy, increased technology and innovation, and the ability of foreign nations to copy U.S. business and manufacturing methods. It may also be that the educational systems of other nations are catching up to the United States and that is a primary reason other nations are challenging the U.S. economy. It is not so much that the U.S. educational system is in decline as it is that other nations are doing a better job of mass public education, teaching critical thinking skills, and preparing students for college and the job marketplace. U.S. schools are the envy of the modern industrial world and we should be flattered that other nations are imitating our methods of public education (NCES 1997).

According to the U.S. Department of Labor, Bureau of Labor Statistics, increases in educational attainment were responsible for an estimated 11 to 20 percent of growth in worker productivity in the United States in recent decades. Increases in high school graduation rates are not the only factor in worker productivity. For example, "increases in capital accounted for an estimated 40 percent of growth in worker productivity in the United States from 1948 to 1990" (U.S. Department of Labor 1992, pp. 1–2).

Successes of education over the past fifty years include increasing the high school graduation rate to nearly 87 percent (although many researchers are skeptical of this high percentage rate when drop-out statistics are considered

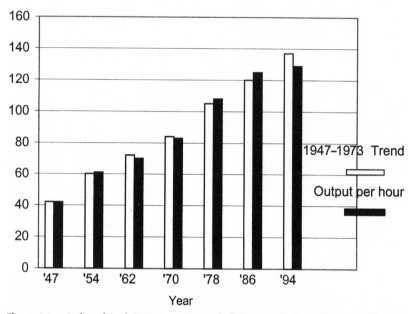

Figure 1.2.   Index of Real Output per Hour of All Persons, Business Sector: 1947–1994
Note: Hours of all persons include hours of employees, proprietors, and unpaid family workers. Output
    is the constant-dollar market value of final goods and services produced.
Source: U.S. Department of Labor, Bureau of Labor Statistics. *Handbook of Labor Statistics,* Washington,
    D.C.: U.S. Government Printing Office, August 1995.

[Holland 2003]), sending 64 percent of high school graduates on to college
with the highest Scholastic Aptitude Test (SAT) and American College Testing (ACT) scores in history, and providing vocational programs for millions
of students (NCES 2004c). In the twenty-first century, we will continue to
graduate nearly all our students from high school and send millions of well-
qualified students to college. There are other needs in the marketplace, however, besides college graduates. We also need skilled workers (Harris, Handel, and Mishel 2004). The question is, will the cutting of vocational training
programs from our schools handicap a large segment of our secondary
school students? Will increasing the number of college graduates overcome
the need for skilled workers in nonprofessional occupations? We are pro-
gressing on one hand and handicapping ourselves on the other. We may be
forcing failure on a significant portion of our population and will experience
a labor shortage of skilled workers at the same time. Current policies coming
out of No Child Left Behind, the Carl D. Perkins Act grant awards, and other

governmental education programs seem to acknowledge we are headed in that direction.

LOGICAL CONCLUSIONS ABOUT EDUCATION AND ECONOMIC PROSPERITY

Why is it that those responsible for setting public policy for education in the United States are focusing most of the funds earmarked for education and most of the attention on the college bound? Is that really the most economically thoughtful thing to do? Would not spending at least as much on programs like school-to-work, tech prep, and job apprenticeships mean as much to worker productivity and the economy as a whole as helping students receive better scores in algebra, geometry, and American literature? Although being concerned about providing opportunities and training for the college bound is certainly important, isn't providing opportunities and vocational training in high school for the noncollege bound equally as important?

Educators and those who set educational policy must not succumb to the elitism inherent in the "everyone must go to college" myth. Even the most elitist legislator or local representative would be hard-pressed to say that the occupations listed above for ninety million jobs that do not require a college degree are less important to the economy than highly skilled technical jobs.

We are a democracy and a democracy means that all the people, not just the college educated, are created equal. All people are deserving of the pursuit of happiness. Just look around you as you drive through your community and count the number of people doing important work for the community who do not need a college education: the people who collect your trash, the mailperson, the mechanic in the gas station, the telephone repair worker, the truck drivers, the gas station attendants, the clerks at the cleaners, the waitresses, and the cooks. Do those types of jobs really need advanced algebra and geometry?

It is time for public policy makers to treat all citizens equally. Everyone who pays taxes and lives in the United States deserves an equal share of the privilege of citizenry. *Success* is a word that means a favorable outcome or result. That favorable outcome does not necessarily mean wealth or a high and lofty position. It could mean success in your job, whatever it is. It can also mean being an excellent parent or family member, or striving to become whatever it is you want to become. To equate a college education with the only way to achieve success is wrong and somewhat deceitful. We need to take a second look at some of our decisions and directions related to public and private education in the United States.

2

FOUR CASE STUDIES

L ooking at real-life examples is always a good way to make the transfer from theory to reality. The following four case studies will perhaps provide insight into the lives of four young people who could make the statement "College is not for me." As you read each case study, see if the young people involved remind you of someone you know.

ANGELA

Angela is seventeen years old. She lives in East Los Angeles, California. She is a first-generation Mexican American. Her mother went to school until the eighth grade and her father until the tenth grade in Mexico. She has one sister and a brother. She lives with her parents in a modest three-bedroom house in a neighborhood that is at least seven decades old. Her neighborhood is very close to downtown Los Angeles. Her father works the graveyard shift at a meatpacking plant in nearby Vernon. Her mother cleans houses twice a week and takes the Big Blue Bus to the neighborhoods where she cleans houses in nearby Beverly Hills. Angela goes to Roosevelt High School in East Los Angeles. Roosevelt High School is an old school built in 1925 and its student population is 80 percent Latino. Roosevelt High School is a comprehensive high school in the Los Angeles Unified School District and has a wide range of course offerings preparing students to go to a two-year or four-year college. Because of budget constraints, elective courses in vocational subjects have been limited to typing, computer operation, and child care.

Angela has no interest in academic subjects but she manages to get C grades in history, English, and general math classes. Her favorite class is physical education. She has a boyfriend who is older and out of school. He graduated from Roosevelt High School two years ago and now works as a carpenter. Angela is thinking seriously about dropping out of school. She could get her GED and go to work somewhere. Her parents think that it is a good idea since she has so little interest in school. Her boyfriend thinks she should finish high school and then get a job. Angela is an attractive young woman with bright brown eyes, olive skin, and a pleasant smile. She likes to wear her hair in a large upswept style that is popular with many Mexican girls in East Los Angeles, and likes to put a purple streak down the middle of her hairdo. She also spends a great deal of time on her fingernails. They are painted many different colors depending on her mood. Her favorite hobby is working on her friend's hairdos. She loves styling and combing hair to fit a person's face, and Angela likes to cut her boyfriend's hair as well. Mixing the colors to dye her friends' hair is sometimes a challenge, and she wishes she knew more about dyes and what makes them work. She has very few tools to work with but her parents bought her an expensive set of combs for her last birthday.

There is a beauty college in downtown L.A. that Angela would like to attend, but it is expensive. It costs $500 for each class and she needs seven classes in order to receive her beautician's license. She knows that many beauty shops do not require a beautician's license but the best and highest-paying shops do. Cleaning houses like her mother seems to be the only way she can earn the money to pay for beauty school. In order to clean houses, she would have to quit school. This seems to be the only way. If she doesn't follow this path, she is afraid she will either flunk out of school because of boredom or get pregnant like her sister. On one level, she would like to finish high school and get her high school diploma and have her parents see her go across the stage at graduation. She would be the first person in her family to graduate from high school. On the other hand, it isn't worth the boring classes where teachers continually drone on about how important it is to go to college. Angela isn't certain she wants to finish high school, let alone college.

ROBERT

Robert is going to be eighteen years old in July. He lives on the north side of Philadelphia, not too far from the river. He is African American. He has been a good but not excellent athlete in high school. Many of his friends are going to college on football or basketball scholarships. He is not really that interested in playing sports but did so in high school because of his friends. His real interest is making money. He likes the things that money can buy: nice clothes, cars, and so on. He lives with his mother and two sisters in a two-bedroom apartment. It is not a bad neighborhood, just poor. He is not certain where his father lives. He sees his father about twice a year, usually around Christmas or in the summertime. His mother works as a clerk in a pharmacy not too far from their house. His two sisters are older but still live at home. He sleeps on a foldaway sofa bed in the living room. They are a happy family, and overall, life has been stable and good. Robert's biggest problem is that he does not like school. He hates to read, although he reads fairly well. He likes math but hates algebra. He has learned how to type but does not have a computer, nor does he want one. He attends North Side High School, which is a comprehensive high school. There are magnet schools he could apply for but they focus primarily on science or technology. He is not interested in either. Robert receives Cs and Ds in school with the exception of physical education, where he receives an A. He works part time as a stock boy in a liquor store. He does not like the work but he likes the wages he receives. He spends most of his money on clothes and likes to think he is one of the best-dressed guys in school. Robert has mixed feelings about graduating from high school but he probably will because it is easier to graduate than to drop out. He has friends who have dropped out of school and attendance counselors or police types continually follow them around. Robert hates being hounded, so he will probably follow the easy way out and graduate. He has no idea what he wants to do after high school.

Robert has great social skills—his mother says he could make friends with an iceberg. He has a great smile and a good sense of humor. He likes to be enthusiastic and positive. He has always liked people. His mother frequently talks about how rude people are in the store she works in and how much she hates it. Robert is good at basic math and he can easily solve word problems that involve practical situations.

The one thing that interests Robert after high school is a sales job. If he could only get the right kind of job where he could wear nice clothes and sell something he believed in, he knows he could make a lot of money. The trouble is, most of the sales jobs he has heard about pay minimum wage. There could be an opportunity to work for Mr. Langley at the liquor store after he graduates but he can't sell liquor until he is twenty-one. Working stock for three more years seems just plain boring. If only he could find a way to sell cars! That is something that would fascinate him. He does not really know anything about cars, and none of his friends or family have a car. He takes the Metro when he wants to go downtown. He has never traveled outside of Philadelphia but television has shown him that there is a whole world out there that he wants to experience. That takes money and he has none.

BETH

Beth is sixteen years old, blonde, overweight, and has always had trouble with schoolwork. She lives in a little rural town not too far from Pierre, South Dakota. Her dad works as a farmhand in the summer and fall and is usually out of work in the winter and spring. Her mother is a housewife and has never worked. They have very little money and sometimes have to take food stamps during the winter and spring. She has a nine-year-old little brother whom she hates. She attends Willow Brook Union High School, which is nearly twenty miles away. She travels two hours each day on the school bus in order to get to school and back. She hates the kids on the bus. She hates most of the kids at school. Most of all, she hates her teachers—there is not one of them she really likes. She has one good friend, Sally, whom she knows from church. Sally hates school too. Beth manages to get C grades in most of her classes. She never does her homework but her classes are easy and she only needs to attend in order to get a C.

One thing Beth likes is her church. She does not understand half of what the minister is talking about but that is OK because she likes the singing and she likes the overall atmosphere. Both her mother and father go to church. Her family is pretty religious, and saying grace before every meal is a regular ritual, as is a weekly prayer meeting at their house. Her friend Sally (who is not religious) often makes fun of Beth, telling her she is a "Holy Roller." Beth takes Sally's kidding good-naturedly and says she is just jealous.

Beth also loves children. She is very good with children. Everyone says so. She often volunteers for child care at her church. She does not like to miss the church service but working with the children makes her feel good. Actually, it makes her feel better than about anything else she can think of. She likes to see the children laugh and play. She loves to read to them. People often compliment her about being good with kids. She knows she is. She can make them behave, laugh, and get along with each other better than anyone else at church. She would love to have children of her own someday but she's not certain that is in the cards for her—still, you never know.

Beth is not certain what she wants to do after high school. Nothing really interests her. She has tried to learn to type but did not do very well. She hates reading and math. She hates social studies most of all. The fact that she is so overweight hinders her ability to do well in physical education. Teachers are always talking about going to college or planning for the future. She has no idea about her future. Maybe something will come along. She wishes there were classes in child care at her high school. Her Aunt Jossie said they used to have such classes when she went to high school.

SETH

Seth is seventeen and lives in the suburbs of Raleigh, North Carolina. He lives with his father in a small two-bedroom house in a poor neighborhood. His mother died when he was five years old and his dad and he get along pretty well. His father is a long-distance truck driver and is not home for long periods of time. Seth has learned to cook for himself and actually is a pretty good cook. He likes to make spaghetti and meatballs. His dad loves eating Seth's cooking when he is home.

Seth receives excellent grades in school. All his teachers and counselors say he is college material. He likes to read, and does especially well in math, computers, and history. He is also a pretty good athlete but has no interest in playing sports. Seth also has no interest in going to college. For one thing, they do not have the money to send him there, and he heard it costs a lot of money. For another thing, the idea of sitting in a classroom any longer than he has to makes him sick to his stomach.

The thing that Seth really likes to do is work on cars. His uncle has two old vehicles that he lets the kids in the neighborhood work on. His Uncle Bill has all the tools he needs and the area behind his garage has a block and tackle hooked up so they can pull engines when they need to. Seth and two of his friends actually often ditch school when they are at a particularly interesting task of rebuilding an engine. They usually go to school when they have no more money to buy parts. Spare parts are hard to come by and they often have to work after school at the local nursery, caning roses, in order to earn the money to go into Raleigh to the wrecking yards to search for parts. They do not know what they are going to do with the cars when they are finished. Probably his uncle will help them sell them so they can have some money to go to the prom. Actually, they like working on the cars more than they like girls, but the prom seems like something they should do.

There is a new car dealership in town that is advertising for mechanics. The problem is, being a mechanic in a new dealership means he has to know how to use complicated analysis machines. Seth has no idea how to even approach learning how to use the analysis machines. There are no schools in the area that could teach him and certainly his high school, which prides itself on sending 75 percent of its students to college, has no classes to teach him. He has heard of schools called "trade schools" but there are no trade schools near his home. There is a community college but it mostly provides classes for kids to transfer to North Carolina State or Duke. It doesn't have classes on automobile engine analysis anyway. He is not interested in anything the community college has to offer. There used to be a program called "tech prep" at his high school but that program is now called "career and technical education," and students have to have a B average and take algebra, geometry, chemistry, and physics in order to get into the program.

Seth figures he'll probably go to work as a truck driver like his dad. There is absolutely nothing wrong with driving trucks. It pays well and the Teamster's Union provides lots of benefits. It just is not the thing that fills him with passion. Working on cars does that for him. Perhaps he can fill his passion by working on his own car once he gets one. Maybe he'll quit school, get his GED, and find a way to earn enough money to buy his own car.

SOUND FAMILIAR?

Most parents or educators reading the four case studies above know at least one of these kids. They are not unusual. Good, solid kids, from good families, who want what we all want—a good job and a future filled with positive experiences. Most of all, we want a job that we like. The problem that we see in all four scenarios is that they are probably going to be frustrated in their desires. School does not provide them with what they need or want. For all four of these young people, school is geared toward the college educated. No one seems to want what he or she wants. It is somewhat sad, isn't it? There is no one to give them help or advice. The saddest part is that the scenarios are so real. It would not take that much to help these adolescents reach their dream.

3

THE MYTH
OF ALGEBRA

For many people, algebra has become the holy grail of entrance into the world of academics. Legislators, business leaders, and even some learning psychologists have praised the ability of mathematics to serve as a path to a better-educated, better-performing, and better-prepared workforce. Some have indicated that without the proper exposure to mathematics, students are doomed to failure in the world of work. Algebra in particular has been included in graduation exit exams and other measures of student academic progress. Instruction in algebra for everyone has been cited as a civil rights issue. Since colleges and universities require algebra as an entrance requirement, some say that to deny students algebra is to deny them access to college.

Louis V. Gerstner Jr., chairman and CEO of IBM, is an example of how a business leader can promote algebra and math as a stepping-stone to success. In his book *Reinventing Education* he states, "A recent study by the College Board revealed that students of all races and backgrounds who take both algebra and geometry are almost equally likely to attend college!" (Gerstner et al. 1994, p. 65). In today's high-tech world, these are the gatekeeper courses for science, engineering, medicine and allied health fields, and computers. This is certainly an important and probably true statement for the college bound. Then, Mr. Gerstner makes a quantum leap in his thinking when he says, "Without knowledge of algebra and geometry, today's student is tomorrow's failure" (Gerstner et al. 1994, p. 65). This is a good example of the type of thinking that permeates the thinking of many politicians, legislators, and businesspeople. Can we really say that students who do not go to college or who do not take algebra and geometry are doomed to failure?

Just what is algebra and does it really help prepare people to think? Should we require it of all students because of its critical thinking and job preparation importance? Should algebra be included in graduate exit examinations required of all students? These are very important questions because if the answer is "yes" to all three questions, the curriculum of our schools and student preparation will be indelibly affected. This chapter hopes to provide insight into these important questions.

WHAT IS ALGEBRA?

In order to answer the question "What is algebra?" we need to ask, "What is mathematics?" because algebra is a branch of mathematics. Keith Devlin, in his book *The Math Gene* (2000), makes a clear distinction between arithmetic and mathematics. Arithmetic is the manipulation of numbers. Arithmetic makes calculations such as addition, subtraction, division, and multiplication. Arithmetic is very different from mathematics. Devlin describes mathematics as "the science of patterns. The patterns can be real or imagined, visual or mental, static or dynamic, qualitative or quantitative, utilitarian or recreational. They arise from the world around us, from the depths of space and time, and from the workings of the human mind" (p. 11). He goes on to say that there are different branches of mathematics such as calculus (patterns in motion), geometry (patterns in shape), probability theory (patterns of chance), and algebra (patterns in addition and multiplication). Modern abstract algebra is only about 150 years old and is therefore one of the newer disciplines.

Mathematicians tell us that the use of symbols is crucial to their field. The symbols provide an abstract knowledge of patterns that allow mathematicians to think about, manipulate, and communicate a concept. Some have said that mathematics is a language but that may be too simplistic. Mathematics is more than just language. It is an entire way of thinking about the universe. It is also very abstract. To be able to really understand mathematics means that you have an ability to understand abstractions. Mathematics often uses symbols instead of numbers or words. An example would be that it does not matter in what order numbers are added: $a + b = b + a$.

For someone who is unusually astute in mathematics, symbols resonate like notes on a scale and they see the patterns that evolve by the patterns of unknown symbols. For persons without the special talent of seeing patterns in symbolic logic, the symbols are merely objects to be manipulated without any real understanding as to what they represent. For many (if not most) people, the symbols used in algebra do not mean much other than objects to be manipulated in order to solve a puzzle. For the mathematician, symbols mean much more.

Most people have an ability to do numeration; that is, the ability to distinguish between a number of objects. Most of us know the difference between one and a few, single and several, a pair and a dozen. We understand from an early age how to count. But do we really understand the meaning of "oneness" or that some types of numbers do not reflect reality? We are able to think logically when one fact leads to another. But the difficulty lies when a fact is not really a fact but only an idea that we treat as a fact. We treat the fact as though it really exists. For example, no one has really seen "two-ness" in the universe. The idea of two stands for more than one but *two* is only a word. We use the number as if it was a solid, when actually it is only a symbol.

The mathematically talented mind understands the relativity of symbols. Mathematicians use symbols and understand that they are using them in a relative sense of reality. This is a major difference from the way in which most people use mathematical numbers. Numbers for most of us reflect reality and we like to use them to make us feel both intelligent and psychologically safe. After we balance our checkbook each month, we want to be assured that the numbers reflect reality.

Suzanne K. Langer, in her classic studies of symbolism, states, "A mathematician does not profess to say anything about the existence, reality, or efficacy of things at all. His concern is the possibility of symbolizing things, and of symbolizing the relations into which they might enter with each other. ... It is entirely at the discretion of the scientist to say let x mean this, and let y mean that" (Langer 1973, 19). All that mathematics determines is that x and y must be related thus and thus, and not that x and y exist as entities. No mathematician has ever really seen a number; what they have seen is a symbol for a number. Engineers in particular treat numbers as if they were real things. The use of abstractions is the true difference between engineering mathematics and pure mathematics.

Jean Piaget (Piaget and Inhelder 1958), the great cognitive psychologist, wrote a great deal about humans' unique ability to acquire symbols. He states that the ability to form symbols is an achievement of great magnitude. Other animals may create symbols but they are not anywhere close to the level of sophistication as those of humanity. Piaget states that symbols permit people to transcend limitations of space and time. Humans use symbols to "accommodate" what they see, hear, and sense in a manner that they can communicate to others. They "describe" their reality to someone else. This is the way in which humans use numbers and mathematical symbols—as a way to describe their reality. They also use symbols for logic sometimes called "symbolic logic" as a method of providing insight into structures and how they operate.

Keith Devlin tells us,

> The human brain is nine times larger than is normal for a mammal of our body size. It varies between 1,000 and 2,000 cubic centimeters, with the vast majority of us having between 1,400 and 1,555 cubic centimeters. Within this range there is no obvious correlation between size and intelligence. Some very intelligent people have brains of around 1,000 cubic centimeters, and others who show no signs of what we would call high intelligence possess 2,000 cubic centimeters. (Devlin 2000, 13)

Too much has been said by teachers and parents about a child not having the brain to do math. We popularly talk about math intelligence as if it had something to do with inherited brain size. Devlin states that there really is no math gene any more than there is a literature gene or a science gene. The ability to do mathematical problems is much more complex than any isolated gene or group of genes.

THE VOCABULARY OF ALGEBRA

Algebra has a vocabulary peculiar to itself. The vocabulary of algebra is key to understanding the methodology and strategy involved in algebraic problem solving. It also demonstrates the abstractness of the discipline. Common terms used in algebra and their definitions are listed below:

Binomial: an expression containing exactly two terms.

Deductive reasoning: syllogistic reasoning from general to specific.

Dependent variable: used in statistics to indicate that other numbers or variables may influence a number.

Equation: the use of numbers to mean two expressions set equal to each other.

Exponent: a symbol written above and to the right of a mathematical expression to indicate the operation of raising to a power

Independent variable: used in statistics to indicate a number stands alone and is not influenced by other variables.

Inductive reasoning: syllogistic reasoning from specific to general.

Irrational number: a number that can be written as a decimal but not as a fraction.

Linear equation: an equation whose graph of solution forms a straight line.

Monomial: an expression containing one term.

Polynomial: an expression containing more than one term.

Quadratic equation: a method of problem solving using factoring, a quadratic formula, and the completion of squares.

Rational number: any number that can be expressed as a decimal, fraction, or ratio.

Reciprocal numbers: one of a pair of numbers whose product is one.

Variable: a letter used to represent a number.

Each of the above terms is used in the Algebra I, California Standards Test, which was adopted by the California State Board of Education on October 9, 2002. The terms and the California Standards Test are typical of items included in most state testing programs.

A simple question needs to be asked of parents and schoolteachers. When was the last time you solved a quadratic equation? Probably the last time you took a math course, which may have been in high school. When was the last time you drew a straight line using a linear equation? What about solving a problem for two unknowns? Actually for many of us, mathematics is fun and you may have enjoyed those tasks. The reality, however, is that these are problem-solving tasks that you do not use in everyday life unless your profession specifically calls for it. You could make a case for studying mathematics in order to do inductive and deductive reasoning, but you do that with common sense, not with mathematics. You can say, "Most white cats are deaf, my cat is white, therefore my cat is probably deaf." You reason that syllogism with words, but do you really need mathematics to help come to a solution? You can state deductively that if a is true and b is equal to a, than b is also true. Does substituting letters for words really help you think better? Substituting variables for words has good reason in the world of mathematics, but is it really necessary in real life? In reality, there is great controversy in the field of logistics as to whether the use of syllogism is an appropriate way to teach logic. Too much depends on the truth of the basic premise, which may be biased or just plain wrong. We have plenty of examples in the area of world affairs in recent years.

When you closely examine the real purpose of algebra, you need to ask: "Why do students who are not going on to college need algebra?" Is it really necessary as a way to teach them to think? Can they not learn to think deductively and inductively through practical problem solving? It is difficult to think of an automobile mechanic or a hair stylist not having to solve practical problems. Repairing an electrical circuit problem in an ignition system or attempting to mix dyes in order to arrive at a certain color of hair requires difficult and complicated problem-solving tasks that do not involve algebra. A mathematician could probably state the problem symbolically, but why bother? Mathematics is not necessary for the common tasks that an auto mechanic or a hairdresser needs to solve. Why waste time and perhaps boredom and frustration by requiring all students to learn algebra?

MATHEMATICS BLOCKING

There are people who are intelligent in every way except when it comes to mathematics. Mathematics demands the use of abstraction. Although all people who use language have mastered a high level of abstraction, some people cannot apply abstract reasoning to mathematics. It is somewhat of a puzzle as to why this occurs. It could be environmental conditioning on the part of a role model, a parent, or society as a whole (e.g., the myth that girls do not do as well in mathematics as boys). It may have something to do with the inability to see relationships. Some people may be more talented than others in seeing relationships between numbers and symbols, just as some people can draw better than others.

Consider an example of state mathematics standards. The three primary headings listed in the California Content Standards for Algebra I are:

- *Students identify and use the arithmetic properties of subsets of integers and rational, irrational, and real numbers, including closure properties for the four basic arithmetic operations where applicable.* Certainly knowledge and use of mathematics is an important learning tool for engineers, physicists, chemists, and mathematicians, but is it necessary for an auto mechanic or a hairdresser?

- *Students use and know simple aspects of a logical argument.* Certainly this is important for all students, but the question is, can this be taught in English or social studies class better than through mathematics? Mathematical logic is tedious and a very roundabout way to teach deductive and inductive reasoning. Word sentences rather than variables and equations are a much more efficient way to teach logic. Mathematical logic is fine for the physicist or engineer, but why use it for all students when there are easier and more direct ways to teach the same thing?

- *Students use properties of the number system to judge the validity of results, to justify each step of a procedure, and to prove or disprove statements.* For an auto mechanic, the validity of results to justify a procedure is measured by whether the car he or she is working on runs properly. He or she does not need numbers as proof. Hairdressers do not need to use numbers to measure whether customers like the appearance of their hair after haircuts or coloring. In both cases, evaluation measures are immediate and obvious. To use algebraic proofs to solve everyday problems is a waste of time and effort for most people in most jobs and professions.

WHERE IS THE EMPHASIS ON ALGEBRA COMING FROM?

The current emphasis on algebra for everyone probably comes from several origins. One of the origins may be from college-educated professionals and decision makers who somehow view discipline as the best way to train the mind. It is nearly as if the old concept of the human brain reacting like a muscle is still alive and well. After all we have learned about the physiology of the human brain and the various functions of different lobes, so it is possible that there are some people who think the brain reacts like a muscle and you can build it up through mental exercise.

Similarly, some of these same college-educated policy makers are admirers of the word *discipline*. Discipline has to do with behavior, not the thinking process. The idea that you can "train" the human brain is not consistent with what we know about how the brain operates. The human brain is a very complex organ, capable of many things, but training behavior patterns occurs at a very low level of human response. The human brain is capable of infinitely more than training responses. One wonders whether education policy makers have fallen into the trap of the logical theorists. Can policy makers possibly deductively think that because they took algebra in school and did well in life, all children should take algebra? That is a faulty axiom if there ever was one! They could also use inductive logic that would indicate that because a great many successful people have taken algebra, it follows that all people need algebra to be successful. Another faulty axiom. Obviously, many successful people have never even heard of algebra.

Perhaps the best way for policy makers to improve their perspective about algebra for everyone is to talk to the people they know and meet. If they would only ask their friends, "When was the last time you solved a quadratic equation or graphed a linear equation?" Ask the checker at the grocery store, the mailperson, your barber, or a cook in your favorite restaurant if they took algebra in school; do they ever use algebra? To repeat, this is not to say that there are not engineers, physicists, and math teachers who use algebra all the time and whose professions require algebra. The question is, should algebra be required of everyone in school?

There is also the subtle mind-set that believes that algebra is kind of a rite of passage. Some people might say to themselves, "Because I suffered through algebra, you should suffer too." It is not fair to mathematics that some people see math as something you have to "suffer through." Mathematics has brought humanity some of its greatest achievements. Without mathematics, we would not have the foundation and language of modern science. Mathematical reasoning at its highest level brought us some of our greatest thinkers. Actually, for those of us who like mathematics, mathematics is a thing of beauty. Not everyone sees it that way, but no one should ever degrade the study of mathematics. What does deserve criticism is the notion that all students need algebra. Algebra has become a needless and sometimes painful unnecessary hurdle to many students in America. We have to examine whether it is realistic or practical as a requirement.

The civil rights issue about algebra for everyone is a bogus argument. Certainly all students should have the right to take algebra. Students should also have the right *not* to take algebra. Perhaps the core of the argument is that everyone should not have to go to college. If policy makers changed their minds and decided that not everyone should be forced to go to college, then algebra as a requirement would not be necessary. .

4

ACADEMIC ELITISM AND THE NO CHILD LEFT BEHIND ACT

It seemed not so long ago that conservative thinkers in the United States criticized the U.S. Department of Education as providing a home for liberalism and socialism. At one point in his administration, Ronald Reagan attempted to eliminate the U.S. Department of Education. It seems a little strange that President George W. Bush, a conservative, should sign the No Child Left Behind Act (NCLB) into law on January 8, 2002. The No Child Left Behind Act is really an extension of the Elementary and Secondary Education Act (ESEA) that was originally signed into law in 1965 by Lyndon Johnson. The No Child Left Behind Act was supported by both Republicans and Democrats and was easily passed by both houses of Congress. To be critical of NCLB is to be critical of ESEA and all that Title I has accomplished for children living in poverty, children with disabilities, and children who need extra help in beginning to read. The Head Start program, part of ESEA, is one of the most successful programs ever initiated by the U.S. Department of Education, and the statistical results are irrefutable.

The problem areas for NCLB are going to be the same ones ESEA had when it first became law. Lots of prescriptions, but few funds to entice states and local districts to meet the standards proposed. No educator is going to suggest that high standards for student programs, greater expectations of schools and teachers, and establishing benchmarks for evaluation are not good things for education. Lofty goals are not a bad thing as long as there are practical ways to accomplish them. There are school districts, however, that count on Title I funds to meet their budgets, and to deny them funds for underprivileged or disabled children because they did not meet certain academic benchmarks is unfair. Those types of denials are now being corrected by the U.S. Department of Education (Olson 2004b; Popham 2004). Many school districts that are having difficulty meeting goals are schools in poverty areas or schools with large minority immigrant student populations.

Educational policy makers who hope to improve schools through goal setting and evaluation deserve the benefit of the doubt when it comes to good intentions. Their good intentions become misguided, however, when the terms *academic* and *college for everyone* come into the picture. Webster's dictionary defines the word *academic* as "relating to a school of higher learning." Higher education in the United States relates directly to education beyond a high school education. Proposing an increase in academic course work in high school is really proposing the preparation of all students to go to college. Those who would insist on academic learning for all students are, in fact, proposing universal college education for all students. Is that really appropriate in a democratic nation where millions of students have no interest in attending college, let alone have the funds to do so? Why the insistence on college education for all when colleges and university training has primarily been a place to prepare students for specific professions? Are colleges and universities really prepared to accept all students? Will that not destroy the purpose and mission of our system of higher education?

The term *academic subject* has taken on new meaning for many educational policy makers. For them, *academic* means emphasis on reading, math, and science. If that is all that academics means, than there is no problem. Many conservative policy makers mean much more, however, than mere emphasis on reading, math, and science. They mean algebra, geometry, trigonometry, and calculus, as well as being prepared to enter college. They mean taking chemistry and physics and advanced placement (AP) courses in English, U.S. history, and government. Is that type of education appropriate for all students? Should it be forced on students with no interest or aptitude for that type of learning?

The answer, in part, seems to lie in the way in which many people with a college education see the rest of world. If a college education was good for them, they think it must be good for everyone. That is like saying because I speak Spanish fluently, all people should have to learn to speak Spanish. Psychologists call this being egocentric. Egocentrism is the inability to see things from any other perspective but your own. It is also being ethnocentric. Sociologists tell us that ethnocentrism is the attitude that one's belief system is superior to other belief systems. Egocentrism and ethnocentrism are personality characteristics of many of those who are attempting to dictate universal academic college for everyone.

As stated in chapter 1, millions of jobs in this nation do not require a college education. Millions of our fine young people have no interest in academics. Academics are essentially "impractical" by Webster's definition. Academics are rooted in theory, not practicality. Millions of young people prefer a world of work that requires using their hands or completing physical tasks rather than doing abstract mental tasks. Those young people, sometimes inappropriately labeled "blue-collar workers," are no less happy, no less successful, and no less highly striving than those who go on to college to become lawyers, teachers, physicists, or engineers. It is probably true that they will not make as much money as those who go to college, but we all know that money isn't everything. While we are defining things, let us define the term *education*. The word *education* has many definitions, but one of the most commonly accepted one is a change of behavior as a result of experience. What type of experiences do we want for our young people? Most Americans believe in liberty. Liberty involves being able to make choices for oneself. At what age are students able to make their own choices? The Twenty-sixth Amendment to the Constitution allows eighteen-year-olds the right to vote. Most states permit sixteen-year-olds the right to drive an automobile. All states allow young people to legally marry when they are eighteen. Those rights and permissions indicate that we believe that young people can make good choices for themselves once they are sixteen to eighteen years of age. Why not permit high school youth to make their own choices as to whether they want to attend college or not? Why force them into something they do not want to do?

High schools in our nation have traditionally been places where students can make choices. They can choose which courses they want to take and when they want to take them. They can choose whether they want to direct their course work toward college or toward the world of work. They can even choose to prepare themselves for parenthood if that is what they want. They can also choose to participate or not participate in sports, music, drama, or other extracurricular programs. High school is a wonderful world of opportunity and has traditionally been a place for exploration and finding one's potential. Would those who would require universal college preparation really want to destroy the purpose of not only our colleges but also our high schools as well? Will high schools become glorified college-prep academies? Will our colleges and universities have to change their mission statements to accommodate the millions of students who will be forthcoming without an increase in funding from state legislatures? Will the current emphasis destroy the traditional role of the comprehensive high school as a key institution in the maturation process of young adults?

In general, Americans favor more fairness and equality in national life. Most Americans want to live decently, have a chance to get ahead, and be spared arbitrary treatment, whether by business, government, or anyone else. Do our children deserve anything less than the average American?

The authors of such bogus reports as *A Nation at Risk* (National Commission on Excellence in Education 1983) and other criticisms must not seduce educational policy makers. Our schools have not failed this nation. We should be proud of our schools; they are the envy of the world. Our schools have helped this nation become one of the most prosperous nations in the history of the world. Where is the assumption that somehow our schools are failing us coming from?

Much of the current criticism and mistaken notion that our schools have failed us originates from a report entitled *A Nation at Risk*, published in 1983 by the National Commission on Excellence in Education (NCEE). The NCEE cited forty-one commissioned research papers and seven public hearings as the basis for its conclusions in *A Nation at Risk*. None of those papers related to the role of education in the economy. Economists wrote none of the research papers, yet the commission argued that schools were hurting the economy. The report indicated that our once-unchallenged preeminence in commerce, industry, and science is being overtaken by foreign competitors throughout the world. The reason for the progress of foreign competitors was not credited to the progress of foreign schools, but instead was blamed on our system of education. It seemed as if every failure of business or government was being blamed on schools.

There are few real facts cited in *A Nation at Risk*. Instead of evidence, the authors relied on public hostility toward schools in the aftermath of desegregation (Forgione 1998). Instead of crediting other nations for imitating our system of public education as a reason for their progress, the critics looked for a scapegoat for the failure of innovation in manufacturing and industry, and that scapegoat was public schools. Some supporters of the No Child Left Behind Act are echoing much of the report today. There are the same type of arguments that students are not meeting the needs of industry and millions of students are functionally illiterate. There are few statistics or long-term and short-term research studies to support their criticisms. Anecdotal examples of failures—usually involving inner-city schools, whose failures are actually based more on poverty than pedagogy—are used as signposts that our educational system is in trouble. The reality is that our school systems continue to be successful and full of promise.

The U.S. Department of Education, National Center for Educational Statistics, is an excellent resource of factual information to reveal what our schools have accomplished and where they are today. Some interesting statistical data from the center that can help our perspective include:

- The percentage of twenty-five- to twenty-nine-year-olds who completed high school by race and ethnicity in 1971 was 81 percent white, 58.8 percent black, and 48.3 percent Hispanic.
- The percentage of eighteen- to twenty-four year-olds who completed high school by race and ethnicity in 2001 was 93 percent white, 87 percent black, and 63 percent Hispanic. This is the highest graduation rate in our history. SAT and ACT scores have been rising steadily over the past twenty years.
- The average number of core subjects in English, social studies, mathematics, and science in high school has increasingly gone up between 1990 and 2000.
- The average number of credits earned in academic subjects has increased between 1990 and 2000.
- The number of earned credits in computer-related vocational courses has increased every year between 1990 and 2000.

- From 1990 to 2000, the grade point average (GPA) of high school graduates increased from 2.68 in 1990 to 2.94 in 2000.
- In 2000, high school graduates who took AP and/or international baccalaureate (IB) courses in both mathematics and science earned an overall mean GPA of 3.61.
- There are more students entering college than ever before. In 2002, 67 percent of high school students entered some type of higher education.
- Worker productivity in the United States remains among the highest in the world. U.S. worker skills have grown slowly and steadily since World War II. (NCES 1997; Baily and Solow 2001)

Schools cannot take the credit for either economic boom periods or the blame for periods of economic stagnation. Economic cycles are caused by many factors and economists do usually not include education as a significant factor. Blaming education for a poorly trained workforce lacks credibility or factual information to support the premise. Anecdotal information on all sides is easy to come by. Employers who say new employees cannot read or write have actually become few and far between in recent years. That type of criticism was more common in the 1980s than it is today. What criticism that there is today is focused primarily on work habits rather than educational background.

COLLEGE EDUCATION AS A CIVIL RIGHT

But what about the argument that a college education is a civil right and everyone should be prepared to go to college in high school, so that if they make the decision later on that they want to further their education, they will be prepared? That civil right is nearly a given in our present system of education. Certainly, everyone should have the right to go to college if that is his or her choice. But what if that it is *not* their choice? Is it not a student's right not to go to college, if that is their choice? Is that not a civil right as well? Educational policy makers should not force students to fit into a curriculum in which they have no interest. Giving students the right to an education based on reading, writing, and arithmetic is a far cry from forcing students to learn linear equations using two unknowns, understanding the meaning of poems by T. S. Elliot, and memorizing periodic tables. Providing every student with the opportunity to learn to use a computer keyboard is a lot different than teaching them how to write an essay on the contributions of Milton Friedman to the new world economy. Too many college-educated people are obsessed with the idea that a college education is crucial to success. That simply is not true. There are thousands of successful people who did not go to college.

The problem with academic elitists is that success is all about making more money. The idea that being well off may have more to do with liking your job than the amount of money you earn is foreign to many who regard college as the be all and end all to happiness. The very notion that some people may actually like working with their hands is also noxious to many people who see being a blue-collar worker as tantamount to being a failure. Perhaps preparing all high school students for the world of work should be a civil right. Since half the students who begin college drop out during the four years after high school, shouldn't all students be prepared to earn a living without a college education?

At one time in the history of secondary education in the United States, vocational training was a primary purpose of high school. We need to get back to that goal, but we need to include more modern technology. Computers, cell phones, and fax machines are here to stay, and learning to use technology properly has little to do with needing a college education. We can do that in high schools. There is no reason that high schools cannot teach all students to use the basic tools of technology. Insisting that higher education is necessary to learn how to use a computer is a complete exaggeration.

LEGITIMATE CRITICISM

Although there has been much progress in public education over the past thirty years, it does not mean that there is not room for improvement. The drop-out rate for minority students is still much too high (NCES 1999, 2004b). Poverty still exists and millions of students attend crowded, crumbling school buildings. Many teachers are undertrained and underpaid. The problems of distance, isolation, and a lack of resources still affect the quality of education in our rural schools. Educators are still struggling with better ways to deal with the educational needs of special education students. The number of special needs students in our schools is increasing, and the kinds of handicaps being brought into the classroom as a result of fetal alcohol syndrome, different kinds of autism, and attention deficit disorders are stretching the capabilities of many schools and classrooms.

Education is still way too political and is too often used as a scapegoat for other social or economic failures. Factual data, training, and perspective are still the mainstay requirements for those who would make educational decisions; too often, however, research and factual data are ignored in favor of political agendas. There is still no willingness to take advantage of the concepts of multiple intelligence and early identification of talents as proposed by Gardner and others over twenty years ago (Gardner 1983, 2000). School violence and drugs, although rare, are still present in many of our schools (Crosse et al. 2001).

Care must be taken to accept constructive criticism when it is appropriate, but we must be able to tell the difference between elitist slogans and unrealistic goals and the real issues and problems that face our schools, teachers, and school administrators.

THE BIGGEST FEAR

The biggest fear facing many educators today is that those in control of the legislative process will be able to implement an "educate the best and shoot the rest" and "the purpose of public education is to rake the rubies from the rubbish" philosophy. While such a fascist type of philosophy is probably inherent rather than explicit, it may be the underlying thinking that is beneath the surface of many of those who support the No Child Left Behind Act. There may also be a degree of racism lying below the surface. There is no place in America for that type of thinking. We should always suspect hidden racism and prejudice toward immigrants and the poor as possible causal factors when criticism is focused on our schools. Prejudice has been present in our nation since its early beginnings and we need to be suspicious whenever any public institution is criticized.

Our public schools are the pride of the most democratic nation the world has ever known. Fascist-type thinking must not have a place in a public agenda. We want our schools to prepare students to live in a democracy—not a two-tiered system of those who have a college education and those who drop out of school in the eighth or ninth grade and either go on welfare or seek a minimum-wage job for the rest of their life.

The No Child Left Behind Act, properly funded and properly implemented at the state level, can be a positive force for improving our schools. Improperly funded and improperly implemented, it can be an excuse for increasing the haves and have-nots social syndrome that we have today (Rainwater and Smeeding 1995). Although poverty and prejudice still exist in our society, we still have the best economic, social, and educational system known to man. Those who favor elitism over a democratic public school system can destroy our way of life. Any time the federal government tries to tie strings and propaganda to the reserved powers of the states to implement public education, we should rebel. It is fine for the U.S. Department of Education to provide research, special resources for poor children, and scholarships for needy college students, but it is not fine for the federal government to interfere in what is primarily a state responsibility.

Our public high schools are not failing (Jennings and Rentner 2002), and those who say they are have not visited enough schools or talked to enough high school graduates. Too many so-called experts use anecdotal data from high schools in poverty-stricken areas to justify their arguments. Just as all politics is local, we need to ask the general public if they think their local high school is failing. Most communities are proud of their local high school and believe they are doing a good job. They remember their high school lives vividly; while they may not want to relive them, they do not want to deny the same type of experience to their children. High school life as we have known it is an important growing-up experience. Let's not destroy it in the name of some type of elitist philosophy.

5

SCHOOL DROPOUTS, EXIT EXAMS, AND "COLLEGE FOR EVERYONE" PHILOSOPHY

School dropouts have been a concern of parents, teachers, school boards, politicians, and the general public for generations. Fear of what may happen to your child if he or she drops out of school is a legitimate concern. It is a fact that students who drop out of school earn less money than those who finish high school. It is also a fact that school dropouts are more prone to get in trouble with the law, become pregnant, take drugs, and have greater mental health problems. Recent research by the Urban Research Institute Education Policy Center indicates that the national graduation rate is not the widely broadcast 85 percent, but much closer to 68 percent. Minorities nationwide have little more than a fifty–fifty chance of earning a high school diploma (Swanson 2004).

Educators traditionally have done everything they can to prevent students from dropping out of school. The current emphasis on "college for everyone" is endangering many of our students and may be substantially increasing the number of dropouts in this nation. It is a subtle emphasis that may discourage many students who are on the line as to whether to quit school or not. We need to examine some facts and information about school dropouts and what the current emphasis on increased academics for everyone may mean. This is especially important, because many professional researchers and educators believe that poverty is more of a predictor of school success than race, ethnicity, or language spoken in the home. Academic emphasis coupled with poverty may be just too strong a force for many students to endure.

SCHOOL DROPOUTS

Definitions

It is important to keep definitions in mind when we talk about dropouts. Different policy makers use different definitions to justify their positions. If the policy maker wants to praise progress, he or she usually uses the event rate, which is generally a much lower figure. If the policy maker is attempting to make a point for the need for improvement, he or she uses the cohort level which is nearly always much higher. Both sides use high school completion rates, which have multiple uses.

"A dropout is a person 16–19 years old, not in regular school and who has not completed the 12th grade or received a general equivalency degree" (NCES 2004b).

"A drop out is an individual who, according to the school or according to the home and school, is not attending school and has not been in school for four consecutive weeks or more and is not absent due to accident or illness" (NCES 2004b).

"A drop out is an individual who:

1. Was enrolled in school at some time during the previous school year;
2. Was not enrolled at the beginning of the current school year;
3. Has not graduated from high school or completed a state- or district-approved educational program; and
4. Does not meet any of the following exclusionary conditions: transfer to another public school district, private school, or state- or district-approved education program; temporary absence due to suspension or school approved education program; death" (NCES 2004b).

Kinds of Drop-Out Rates

- *Event Rate.* The proportion of students who leave school each year without completing high school. This measure provides information about school retention during the year. The event drop-out rate usually runs around 4 to 5 percent, or about half a million students (NCES 2004b).

- *Status Rate.* The cumulative amount of youths within a given age range who are not in school. This rate would be higher than the event rate since students may have dropped out during a previous year than the event rate and therefore add to the total. In 1998, the status rate was 3.9 million for sixteen- to twenty-four-year-olds, or 11.8 percent of that age group. This rate declined from 14.1 percent in 1980 to 11 percent in 2000 (NCES 2004b).

- *Cohort Rate.* The number of students in a specific grade that drop out over time. It is generally much higher than either the event or status rate. Many school districts do not keep cohort rate statistics so studies are difficult to come by. A longitudinal study done in 2001 by NCES studied a large group of students from when they were in the eighth grade until twelve years later. By 2000, 83 percent of the students in the study had completed a high school diploma. Many large school districts keep cohort rate statistics because capturing student dropouts means millions of dollars to them when funds are tight. The cohort rate in many big-city school districts runs around 40 percent or higher (NCES 2004b).

- *High School Completion Rate.* The number of students in the United States who actually receive a high school diploma or a GED. This has averaged between 85 and 87 percent for the past ten years (U.S. Deptartment of Commerce, 2002).

- *High School Completion through GED or Other Means.* In 1998, two million young adults eighteen to twenty-four years old were reported as having earned high school credentials by passing an equivalency exam such as the GED test (U.S. Department of Commerce 2002).

All of the different drop-out rate definitions are important if we are to talk about the drop-out problem with any meaning or accuracy. When we are talking about how many students drop out of school during any one school year, we are talking about the event rate, which is obviously going to be much lower than the status or cohort rates. The number of transfers coming into a school is usually fairly close to the number of those who transfer out, so you cannot use transience as an excuse for a high status or cohort rate. The high school completion rate is somewhat suspect since it includes students who later received a GED or other certificate before they were twenty-four years old. In some districts, lower-performing students are pushed out of regular high schools and into "alternative educational programs" that they seldom attend for long, and are therefore not counted as dropouts in their regular high schools. There are also students who drop out at the middle school level and never make it to the high school level and are therefore never counted in high school drop-out statistics.

Perhaps the most accurate measure of how many students really drop out during high school is the cohort rate, but that figure is generally not kept. (U.S. Department of Education 2002). Many good high school principals informally know the cohort level for their school. It is not difficult to determine. Just take the number of freshman of a given class and compute the number of who actually graduate four years later and you have the cohort level. Do not be surprised if it is around 25 percent for suburban high schools and 40 percent for urban schools.

The Urban Research Institute Education Policy Center indicates that 1.3 million current ninth graders will leave public high school without earning a diploma. Far too many of those students are members of racial or ethnic minorities (Swanson 2004). Race and ethnicity are often used to emphasize the increased need for drop-out prevention for black or Hispanic students. In 1998, the status drop-out rate for black students was twice that of white students. The status drop-out rate for Hispanics was three times that of white students (U.S. Department of Education 2000).

The statistics for the cumulative effect of dropouts on our society is somewhat shocking.

- In 1998, there were 3.9 million young adults who were out of school yet lacked a high school credential. Overall, 11.8 percent of sixteen- to twenty-four-year-olds in the United States in 1998 were dropouts (U.S. Department of Education 2000).
- Lower economic status has an effect on school drop-out rates. In 1998, young adults living in families with incomes in the lowest 20 percent of all family incomes were four times as likely as their peers from families

in the top 20 percent of the income distribution to drop out of high school (U.S. Department of Education 2000).

- Half of black and Hispanic fourth graders (compared with 5 percent of white fourth graders) are enrolled in schools where 75 percent of the students come from families living at the poverty level. Similarly, about 40 percent of black and Hispanic students attend schools in which 90 percent or more of the students are minorities (U.S. Department of Education 2000).
- Ethnicity also has an effect on school drop-out rates. In 1998, 44 percent of Hispanic young adults born outside the fifty states or the District of Columbia were high school dropouts (U.S. Department of Edcation 2000).
- Latina girls leave high school at a much higher rate than any other group. Teen pregnancy is a major reason why Latina girls leave high school (Vives 2001).

Some progress but still concern.

High school completion rates have increased for white and black young adults since the early 1970s, with rates of 90.2 percent for whites and 81.4 percent for blacks in 1998. Hispanic young adults have not shared in this improvement: 62.8 percent were reported as having completed high school in 1998 (U.S. Department of Education 2000).

Predictable Casualties

Predicting which students are at the greatest risk of dropping out of school is not rocket science. One only needs to look at the statistics. Obviously, the greatest predictor of dropping out of school is poverty. Those who use race or ethnicity as the factor are missing the obvious. If you are black or Hispanic, you have a greater chance of being poor and therefore a greater chance of dropping out of school (Campbell 2003–2004). Race or ethnicity has nothing to do with it; being poor does. Similarly, students who are recent arrivals to the United States have a greater chance of being poor and therefore a greater chance of dropping out of school. The answers to drop-out prevention have to do with economic status, not culture, language, or racial history. If we can raise the economic level of our citizens, the educational level will follow.

Noted demographer Harold Hodgkinson indicates in a recent study that

In 2000, 16.9% of all children in the United States were poor. About one-third of our black and Hispanic children are being raised in poverty, while 10% of non-Hispanic whites live in poverty. However, the largest number of poor children is white, while the highest percentage of poor children are black and Hispanic. Of the 14 million children ages' birth to 18 living in poverty in 2000, 9 million were white and 4 million were black. (Hodgkinson 2003)

The risk factors for children raised in poverty are multifolded. Hodgkinson's study, "Leaving Too Many Children Behind," lists the following risk factors for young children, which have relevance for school drop-out statistics.

- Poverty
- Infant and child mortality
- Low birth weight
- Single parents
- Teen mothers
- Mothers who use alcohol, tobacco, or drugs
- Transience
- Child abuse and neglect
- Lack of quality day care
- Low-wage jobs for parents
- Unemployed parents
- Lack of access to health and medical care
- Low parent education levels
- Poor nutrition
- Lack of contact with English as a primary language

Each factor listed above needs to be examined as a possible causal factor for school dropouts. If educators are going to be in any way sophisticated about causal factors, they have to look at the problem more realistically and avoid superficial surface generalizations. The Luxembourg Income Study of 1995, shown in figure 5.1, illustrates that the United States has one of the highest child poverty rates of any industrialized nation. The United States also has the highest per capita gross domestic product level of any industrialized nation

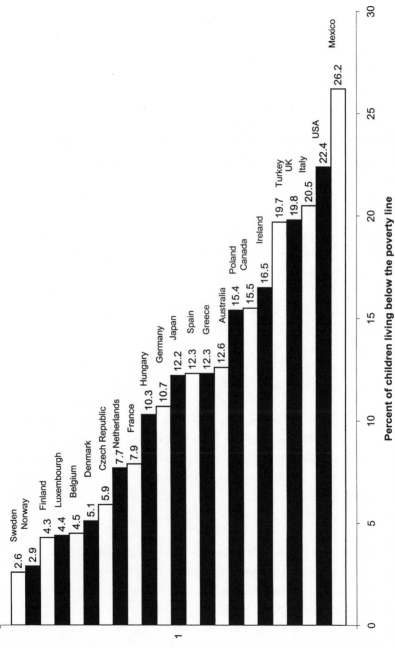

Figure 5.1. Child Poverty in Twenty-Three Developed Countries—Percent of Children Living below the Poverty Line
Source: UNICEF-Innocenti Report Card Issue No 1. 2000.

(*World Almanac Book of Facts* 2005, p. 112). Certainly the United States has the potential to wipe out poverty, which would have a significant effect on the school drop-out problem.

Are higher academic standards and exit exams going to increase the number of dropouts in the United States?

It is still too early to tell. According to the Center on Education Policy, half of public school students attend classes in states with graduation tests, and the number will likely grow to seven in ten students by 2008 (Gayler et al. 2004). Thousands of students failed to receive their high school diploma last year because of "high-stakes tests." Twenty states have diploma-driven exams and five more states plan to administer them by 2009. The tests are different from those required for states to have in place by 2005–2006 under the No Child Left Behind Act. Those tests are not tied to high school graduation. The graduation exams are given at different grades by different states. All states give students more than one time to pass the exam, from two times in New Jersey to eleven times in Minnesota. For states with the exam, students most likely to fail are students in poverty-ridden areas, students with learning disabilities, and those with limited English ability (Futrell and Rotberg 2002).

The Center on Education Policy recently completed a study that indicates that although graduation tests have led to more rigorous courses and more help for struggling students, they have also meant unexpected costs, greater failure rates for minorities, and more dropouts (Gayler et al. 2003, 2004)

A 2004 study by Jay P. Greene and Marcus Winter from the Manhattan Institute for Policy Research entitled "Pushed Out or Pulled Up? Exit Exams and Dropout Rates in Public High Schools" concluded that high school exit exams have no effect on high school graduation rates. While their study is helpful when examining high school completion rates, it fails to determine whether high school exit exams affect cohort rates, which is the real issue at hand. Students may be so discouraged by having to take an exit examination that they do not get to the grade in which the test is administered. That could be even in middle school. It may be true that the number of students who fail exit exams is relatively small but that it may be due to a weeding-out effect of students not getting that far in school.

Another 2004 study done by Walter Haney and colleagues (2004) at the National Board on Educational Testing and Public Policy found that many districts deliberately keep students in the ninth grade for a second year in order to keep them from taking tenth-grade tests. Their study showed there was "a bulge in the education pipeline in the ninth grade" that would indicate more ninth graders than tenth graders nationwide (pp. 176–77).

California delayed the consequences of its exit exam from 2004 to 2006 after a study projected that about 20 percent of seniors would be denied diplomas. In the inner cities, the "don't pass" rate could reach as high as 50 percent. In Massachusetts, where diplomas were withheld for the first time, some students walked out of class and refused to take the test, often with support from parents (Gayler et al. 2003).

The debate over these make-or-break exams is raging around the country, but nowhere is it more intense than in Florida. Nearly 12,800 students— about 9 percent of this year's graduating class—failed the Florida Comprehensive Assessment Test, or FCAT, the tenth-grade-level math and reading exam that students must pass to graduate. Students get six tries on the test between their sophomore and senior years of high school. Many school districts have decided that seniors who failed the test may participate in commencement ceremonies, but may not receive diplomas. Florida officials have not released detailed demographic data on students who failed the test, but preliminary numbers show that about 16 percent of black students and 13 percent of Hispanics flunked, compared with 2 percent of non-Hispanic whites (Gayler et al. 2003).

State Sen. Frederica Wilson (D-Miami) said the program places too much emphasis on a single test. "In minority communities, the one escape from poverty, crime, teen-age pregnancy and drug abuse is education," she said. "If we send our children out into the world without diplomas, what are we saying?" (Amrein and Berliner 2002, pp. 169–72).

Using a test as a method of motivating students is a bad idea. Motivation to learn should be creative, not coercive. Test taking also smacks of putting students into a mold, demanding that everyone come out a certain way. Exit exams may or may not influence the drop-out rate, but educational policy makers need to take a close look as to whether they are helping or hurting education. More research needs to be done to determine whether high school exit examinations discourage students from staying in school. They are probably not a major causal factor. The reasons for dropping out of school are many and exit exams are probably not near the top.

REASONS FOR DROPPING OUT OF SCHOOL

The reasons for dropping out of school are complicated and multifaceted (Abbott et al. 2000). Many of the risk factors for poverty listed by Hodgkinson in his study of neglect and America's youngest children indicated that poverty should probably be right at the top of any list of reasons for students dropping out of school. Poverty, transience, child abuse and neglect, low parent education levels, and lack of English as a primary language need to be seriously addressed as causal factors of school dropouts. Researchers find that dropping out is a process, not an event. It is relatively rare for students to make a snap judgment to leave school. The reasons students leave school, for example, are low grades, inability to get along with teachers or other students, working, pregnancy, and lack of interest in what the school has to offer (U.S. Department of Education 1994).

One of the major reasons many students drop out of school is lack of interest. Over the past two decades, twelfth graders have reported a declining interest in school. Many school reforms over the past two decades have attempted to increase high school students' interest in school (Newman 1992). Despite such attempts, seniors' valuation of their learning activities and self-reports on their efforts do not indicate that higher proportions are more engaged in their schoolwork or trying harder than in years past. Indeed, twelfth graders' interest in school exhibited a decline between 1983 and 2000. The University of Michigan's *Monitoring the Future 12th Grade Study: 1990, 1995, and 2000* indicated that while 40 percent of 1983 seniors said their schoolwork was "often or always meaningful," 28 percent gave this response in 2000. Similarly, the proportion of seniors who said most of their courses were "quite" or "very important in later life" also declined. In addition, students became more likely to take a dim view of school courses over this period: 32 percent of seniors in 2000 said that most of their courses were "very or slightly dull," up from 20 percent in 1983.

The most striking thing about figure 5.2 is the obvious decline of interest in school between 1983 and 2000. Educational policy makers need to ask themselves if anything was happening during those years that could have caused that decline in interest in school. One obvious factor is the decline of courses in vocational education. In the Monitoring the Future study, seniors listed vocational and technical education as the most inter-

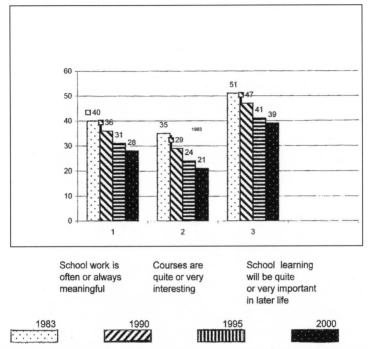

Figure 5.2. Interest in School—Percentage of Twelfth Graders Who Expressed Various Opinions about Their School Experience, 1990, 1995, and 2000

esting as well as the most important subjects offered in school (University of Michigan 2002).

Race and Ethnicity and Dropping Out of School

In our attempts not to be ego- or ethnocentric, it is important to try to attempt to look at things from the point of view of students who are not white or whose parents are not from this country. Points of view might include:

1. "Schools teach things for a white, Anglo-Saxon culture. Schools spend little time teaching me about my culture, race, or background."
2. "There are a lot of economic needs in my family. My mother works two jobs, we get food stamps, and we still have to wear old clothes. Most of the things they teach in school are not going to help earn more money."

3. "I go back to Mexico every summer. One of these days I will not come back to the States. I do not feel I belong there."
4. "I want things now. I want a car, nice clothes, spending money, and things for my baby. School cannot help me get those things."
5. "My mother keeps nagging me to quit school and get a job. She says school is meaningless and there are more important things."
6. "My girlfriend is pregnant and I need to get a job to support her and the baby."
7. "Most of the kids in school have nice clothes, cars, computers, cell phones, and things that I do not have nor can I afford. They make me feel bad and I do not like to be around them."
8. "My people learn by watching, not by reading and telling, and I cannot learn the way the teachers teach in school."

Poorly Financed Schools and Dropouts

School climate is terribly important in drop-out prevention. Schools that are old, dirty, violent, and badly in need of renovation breed dropouts. So do overcrowded classes, poorly trained teachers and administrators, and lack of counselors, tutors, and libraries. School districts need money if they are to effectively prevent school dropouts. Many critics of public schools fail to notice that many schools are crumbling around them but they would rather criticize curriculum than vote for funds that would provide real remedies. Somehow, it is more sophisticated to talk about requiring algebra than new boilers and air conditioning for schools. There is little doubt that additional funding would help schools fulfill their responsibilities. Requiring college for everyone is a big stretch for school districts that are having trouble keeping the doors open.

The GED Test as a Catch Basin

The Graduate Educational Development testing program is often cited as an alternative to a high school diploma. The revised 2004 GED series of tests consists of five sections with a possible 800 points possible. Test takers need a minimum score of 410 on the new test in order to pass. The average age of those who took the GED in 2002 was twenty-five years old. GED Testing

Service indicates that only 1 percent of adults in the United States today have earned a diploma by passing the GED. Passing rates vary greatly by state. More than 96 percent of 2002 test takers in Delaware, for instance, passed the GED, while only 52 percent passed in neighboring New Jersey (Cavanaugh 2004a).

The higher academic expectations being promoted by the No Child Left Behind advocates seem to have influenced the GED test makers. The new GED for 2004 will be much harder than the old one. Many test takers may become discouraged and not take the test, thereby making the GED test opportunity one less opportunity for progress and self-esteem for millions of high school youth. It sometimes seems that there is some type of plot going on to keep nonacademic students in a black hole of expectations.

Special Education Students as Dropouts

The U.S. Department of Education Data Analysis System (2003) indicates there were 2,904,282 students between the ages of twelve and seventeen identified under the Individuals with Disabilities Education Act during the 2002 and 2003 school year. This would be approximately 5 percent of the student population for that age group. Their disabilities included 316,899 as mentally retarded, 304,032 as emotionally disturbed, 1,744,473 as having specific learning disabilities, 144,230 as having speech and language disabilities, and nearly 400,000 disorders listed as "other handicaps." Unless we do a better job of working with this large group of students, the drop-out rate from this identified group will become larger and larger. The loss of vocational education training programs in high schools decreases the opportunity for these students to profit from a high school education. Since so many of this group do not read or write well, nor do they do mathematics well, having academic graduation hurdles only increases their belief that they are failures in school. Finding ways for states to make exceptions for these students in terms of testing requirements is probably less important than keeping vocational programs in schools. These students do have potential but there need to be realistic options. There is currently more interest among advocates of the No Child Left Behind Act who are attempting to help. Proposals are being made in which students' higher expectations fit with the abilities of special education students. The initial requirement that would require all students in grades 3–8 and in high school by 2013–2014 to be at the proficient level on state reading and mathematics tests is highly unrealistic for special education or limited English students. Proposed revisions that would look at yearly progress rather than absolute levels of performance are much more likely to keep more students in school (Olson 2004c).

What Are the Answers to the Drop-Out Problem?

There are no easy answers to the drop-out problem. Since the origins of the problem are so complex, the answers need to be complex as well. Some possible answers include:

- Early identification of student talents and abilities in middle schools
- More prescriptive learning programs for special education students
- Better programs for newly arrived immigrants with language problems
- Parent education programs in the community
- More community mental health programs
- Better-trained teachers in our inner cities
- Improved and more modern facilities
- Early identification of potential dropouts
- Return of vocational counselors and school-to-work programs to their rightful place in schools
- De-emphasis on high-stakes testing.
- Increase the number of regional occupational programs (ROPs) in high schools

These are only a few of the suggestions that can be made to decrease the drop-out problem. Each study on the problem seems to have a different solution. Every community may have a different answer to the drop-out problem. This is probably important, since the problems for one part of the nation may not be the same as those in other parts of the nation. A solution may work in one section of the country but not in another. Inner cities in particular have issues related to poverty, race, and ethnicity that suburban areas may not have. Rural areas may have an entirely different set of problems that relate to distance, family needs, and background. Punishing school administrators for not solving the problem of dropouts is much too simplistic and will provide no answers. Placing too much pressure on school administrators will only increase the number of games being played with the identification of school dropouts and the ways students are being counted. Answers must be found to correctly identify the causes in the home and in the community. Schools can provide only part of the solution. One thing is for certain: raising the bar of academic expectation will not help.

Educators need to be more professional and creative in dealing with the problem. The military has been using the Armed Services Vocational Aptitude Battery (ASVAB) since the 1960s. The high school version is called Form 18/19 and is taken by over 900,000 high school students every year. The test measures arithmetic reasoning, auto and shop information, mechanical comprehension, electronics information, and coding speed. Why can't a scaled-down version of the test be administered to middle school students beginning in the seventh grade in order to identify student talents that are appropriate for the workplace but not necessarily for college academic subjects?

As long as educators are stuck in an academic preferential mode, the drop-out problem will continue. Educators need to think outside the box for new ways to attract and interest students in school. School needs to be made so attractive an option that it can override the many risk factors that currently exist in many of our homes and communities. This is not an easy task—but given the proper resources and creativity, educators can make it happen.

6

WHAT COLLEGES EXPECT

Not since the GI Bill of Rights after World War II has there been more ac-cess to higher education that there is today. In 1963, there were 4.3 mil-lion students enrolled in institutions of higher education. Today, there are over 12 millions students enrolled. Generation Y, the children of the baby boomers, will push college enrollment to new, unprecedented highs. More and more older citizens are returning to college for advanced degrees. Immi-gration has placed an added burden on college and university enrollments (NCES 2004c).

Colleges have a right to expect academic skills that correspond to their mission statement. Colleges are not expected to play the same role as K–12 public schools. The purpose of public education is to take every child as far academically and socially as possible during twelve years of free education. Education is compulsory for all children. Every effort is made to ensure that all children receive a free K–12th-grade education regardless of race, creed, religion, or ethnicity. A K–12 education is deemed to be important if citizens are to be well-informed, capable adults.

Colleges and universities are designed primarily as institutions of higher learning. Although every state has a system of state-sponsored higher educa-tion, most colleges and universities are not free. The number of scholarships available to enter institutions of higher education continues to get smaller and smaller and more and more competitive. Private universities are very expensive and out of reach for most students without scholarships. Community colleges are generally inexpensive but only provide for either the first two years of college education or specialized programs.

College undergraduate programs are designed with an emphasis toward the humanities. The humanities prepare students for the branches of learning that deal with human thought and culture. Undergraduate education usually includes the sciences, mathematics, writing skills, and the social sciences. The humanities include languages, literature, the arts, and philosophy. During the last two years, students begin to specialize in a major field of knowledge. Graduate programs following a bachelor of arts or bachelor of science degree lead to either research or one of the professions. The professions include teaching, journalism, engineering, law, business administration, medicine, dentistry, architecture, and many more. Research fields include any one of the sciences, economics, political science, history, mathematics, engineering, or medicine.

THE SCHOLASTIC APTITUDE TEST (SAT)

The SAT is a test that provides important clues as to what colleges and universities expect for incoming freshman. The new SAT for 2005 will set higher standards for incoming freshman than ever before. With the addition of writing and items from third-year college preparatory math, students will have to demonstrate mastery of more predicted college success skills. Students will need to complete course work in algebra I, geometry, and algebra II in order to score high enough for college admission and success. In addition to math skills, students need to have the recommended skills in the following areas:

- *Writing skills*: Ability to write a well-developed essay that develops a point of view on an issue. Students need to think critically, form their own perspective, and support their ideas with evidence based on their own experiences, readings, or observations. They have sixty minutes to write the essay on the 2005 SAT examination.

- *Paragraph writing and development*: Ability to carefully examine a paragraph of an essay and improve sentence structure, parts of sentences, or word choice. The task is also to organize the entire essay and its organizational structure. In making those revisions, the student is to follow the conventions of standard written English.

- *Critical reading*: Ability to read a short passage of 100 words and a long passage of 500–800 words and answer specific questions about their content. The analysis will take critical reading skills. The student has seventy minutes to complete this section.

- *Mathematics*: Ability to use numbers and operations in algebra, functions, geometry, statistics, probability, and data analysis. The 2005 SAT will include expanded math topics, such as exponential growth, absolute value, and functional notation, and will place a greater emphasis on such topics as linear functions, manipulations with exponents, and properties of tangent lines. Quantitative comparisons will be eliminated beginning in 2005.

- *Numbers and operations*: The new SAT (2005) will include mathematics questions that require knowledge of exponential growth sequences, also called geometric sequences. Real-life applications in areas such as population growth will be required.

- *Data analysis, statistics, and probability*: The new SAT (2005) will ask students to identify the general characteristics of the best fit for a scatter plot. Students will need to determine whether the line has a slope that is positive but less than 1. Students will be expected to be able to interpret data displayed in tables, charts, and graphs (College Board Examinations 2004).

COLLEGE AND UNIVERSITY MISSION STATEMENTS

Every college or university has an explicit mission statement that has been adopted by its board of trustees and is vaguely understood by faculty and students. For most colleges and universities, service is included along with teaching and research as defining the tripartite mission of the institution. The nature of the mission statement and the degree to which it guides policy and decisions evolve over time. Looking at the mission statement from time to time provides university staff with an opportunity of self-examination. Are they fulfilling their mission as stated? If not, can they change their course in order to do so? If they are fulfilling their mission, how can they stay the course? Examining parts of the mission statements of three major universities may be helpful in determining whether mission statements are similar and whether the purpose of a university education fits the needs of all students currently enrolled in high school.

The University of California

The University of California's fundamental missions are teaching, research, and public service.

Teaching

"We teach and educate students at all levels, from undergraduate to the most advanced graduate level. Undergraduate programs are available to all eligible California high-school graduates and community college transfer students who wish to attend the University of California."

In actuality, admission to the campuses of the University of California is limited to approximately 10 percent of graduating high school graduates. Because of overcrowding and limited funding, freshman students are currently being guided to their local community college with the guarantee that they will be admitted their junior year.

Research

"[Research] is done by some of the world's best researchers and brightest students in hundreds of disciplines at its campuses, national laboratories, medical centers and other research facilities around the state."

Public Service

"[Public service] dates back to UC's origins as a land grant institution in the 1860s. Today, through its public service programs and industry partnerships, UC disseminates research results and translates scientific discoveries into practical knowledge and technological innovations that benefit California and the nation" (University of California 2004).

The University of Texas

The mission of the University of Texas System is to provide high quality educational opportunities for the enhancement of the human resources of the State of Texas, the nation, and the world through intellectual and personal growth. This fundamental, comprehensive mission statement applies to the varied elements and complexities of a large and diverse group, of academic and health institutions that, individually, reflect divergent and distinct missions, histories, cultures, goals, programs and challenges. Through one or more of its individual institutions, The University of Texas System seeks:

To provide superior instruction and learning opportunities to undergraduate, graduate, and professional school students from a wide range of social, ethnic, cultural, and economic backgrounds, thereby preparing educated, productive citizens who can meet the rigorous challenges of an increasingly diverse society and an ever-changing world. To engage in high quality research that entails the discovery, dissemination, and application of knowledge.

To render service to the public, which produces economic, technical, social, cultural, and educational benefits through interactions with local, Texas, national and international entities and individuals. (University of Texas 2004)

The University of Wisconsin–Madison

The primary purpose of the University of Wisconsin–Madison is to provide a learning environment in which faculty, staff and students can discover, examine critically, preserve and transmit the knowledge, wisdom and values that will help ensure the survival of this and future generations and improve the quality of life for all. The university seeks to help students to develop an understanding and appreciation for the complex cultural and physical worlds in which they live and to realize their highest potential of intellectual, physical and human development.

[The University of Wisconsin] also seeks to attract and serve students from diverse social, economic and ethnic backgrounds and to be sensitive and responsive to those groups that have been under served by higher education. (University of Wisconsin 2004)

PROFESSORIAL DEMANDS AT COLLEGES AND UNIVERSITIES

Have college and university professors maintained their standards in terms of what they expect of their students? Does the college and university professor have a responsibility to share responsibility for underprepared students? Should they broaden their outcome expectations to ensure that more students graduate? Should instruction correlate highly to the mission of the university or should it be watered down to meet the needs of less-prepared and academically talented students? These are only some of the questions that need to be asked before we continue to insist that all students need to go to college. Current ambitions of elitist educators may not be realistic in terms what a university education is supposed to be all about. Many college professors complain that too many high school graduates come to them unprepared. This is especially true in terms of writing ability. Some professors simply refuse to read essay examinations full of misspellings and grammatical errors. Some professors expect to "wash out" a percentage of their students. To many professors, high academic standards are what college is all about. Many professors believe that academic freedom includes the right to maintain standards that are worthy of an institution of higher education.

THE MISSION OF COMMUNITY COLLEGES

Community colleges today have multiple missions. Although they originated as "junior colleges," by the end of World War II their mission was broadened to serve the needs of the community. Those community needs included preparing police officers, firefighters, real estate brokers, bookkeepers, draftspersons, nurses, and medical technicians. Today, those needs include providing for the academic courses necessary for the overflow of enrollment at public universities. Unfortunately, the demands of the expanding university and college system are pushing vocational and technical education further and further into the background. Soon there will be no room at many community colleges for vocational and technical course work.

Based on national data, enrollments at public four-year institutions increased by 24 percent between 1980 and 2000 (NCES 2002c). Community college enrollments increased by 32 percent during those same years. This expansion is significant because community colleges enroll nearly half of the public postsecondary students in the country and around 37 percent of all postsecondary students. In California alone, the state needs to find room for 700,000 more students in higher education, much of that at the 109 community colleges. There are 1,632,000 students enrolled in community colleges in the state of California, the nation's largest community college system.

Vanessa Smith Morest (Teachers College, Columbia University), in her excellent paper on emerging issues for community colleges, makes this statement: "There is little agreement about the development of the multi-mission community college because interpretation of the sector's social roles is a matter of perspective" (pp. 1–3). A special focus of this discussion has been on the purposes of vocational education. The concurrent democratization of postsecondary education, and the emergence of the vocational mission of community colleges occurred during the 1960s and paralleled the earlier development of the comprehensive high school. At the high school level, it was assumed that not all students are likely to succeed in academic subjects, so schools should provide students with alternative course work that will interest them and ultimately prepare them for life, thereby making their compulsory education more meaningful (Morest 2004).

The reality is that the original mission of the community college is being supplanted by the needs of four-year colleges and universities. State legislatures and boards of trustees must make some rationale for turning away hundreds of thousands of qualified high school graduates. There simply is not room for all the high school students that qualify for college entrance. Even with higher SATs and GPAs, thousands of high school students are continuing to meet the requirements of state colleges and universities. Affirmative action in some institutions has increased the entrance discrepancy. Deans of admissions have no recourse but to refer students to community colleges, with some type of guarantee admission their junior year.

What has happened to the community college as a wonderful time of exploration of vocational options? Taking course work in fire or police science, real estate law, nursing, secretarial skills, plumbing, and electronics have been replaced with traditional lower-division requirements of universities and colleges.

Do the advocates of "every child a college graduate" possibly understand the ramifications of what they are proposing to do to the college, university, and community college system? They cannot possibly comprehend what sending more students would mean to the current system.

INCREASES IN COLLEGE ENROLLMENT

The number of eighteen- to twenty-four-year-olds will grow by three million by 2010; African Americans, American Indians, and Hispanics will make up almost 60 percent of the population increase over that time period (U.S. Department of Education 2003). The children of the baby boomers will push college enrollment to new, unprecedented highs. More and more older citizens are returning to college for advanced degrees. Immigration has placed an added burden on college and university enrollments. There are a total of about 2,500 higher education institutions in the United States that offer four-year degrees. If you factor out specialty institutions, for-profit schools, distance learning outlets, and so forth, there are about 1,400 colleges and universities that meet the general definition of a "regular" four-year college or university. These institutions graduate approximately 90 percent of all undergraduate students.

COLLEGE RETENTION RATES

The American college and university system continues to have a deep-rooted problem related to high completion-failure rates. Only six out of every ten full-time freshmen in four-year colleges and universities receive a bachelor's degree within six years (Berkner and Cataldi 2002). A disproportionate number of those "dropouts" are minority or low-income students. Latino college students drop out of school far more frequently than their white counterparts and earn bachelor's degrees less than half as often. Latinos with the best high school academic backgrounds lag behind whites with similar backgrounds in receiving four-year college degrees. A 2004 report by the Pew Hispanic Center, a project of the University of California

UNDERGRADUATE ENROLLMENT: Total undergraduate enrollment in degree-granting two- and four-year postsecondary institutions (in thousands), by sex, attendance status, and type of institution, with projections: Fall 1970–2012

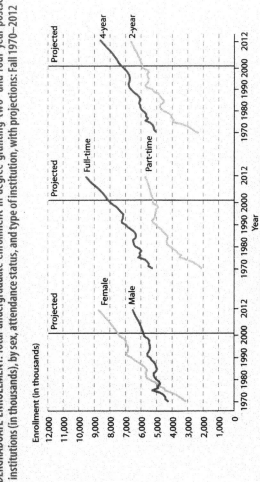

Figure 6.1. Undergraduate Enrollment in Two-Year and Four-Year Postsecondary Institutions

National Center for Education Statistics, U.S. Department of Education, *The Condition of Education 2003*

Annenberg School for Communications, reported that 23.2 percent of Latino college freshmen earn bachelor's degrees by age twenty-fix, versus 47.3 percent for whites.

The six-year retention and graduation rates actually vary greatly by institution. Table 6.1 demonstrates a study done by the University of Kentucky to compare its retention rate with other institutions. About two-thirds of all institutions are in a range running from 35 percent to 70 percent. Nearly one out of five four-year institutions in America graduate less than one-third of their first-time, full-time, degree-seeking freshmen within six years (U.S. Department of Education 2002).

Table 6.1. University of Kentucky and Benchmark Institutions Retention and Graduation Rates

Institution	One-Year Ret. Rate 1996 Cohort	Six-Year Grad. Rate 1993 Cohort
University of Kentucky	78%	53%
North Carolina State University	88%	65%
Ohio State University	79%	56%
Pennsylvania State University	92%	80%
Purdue University	87%	64%
Texas A&M University	88%	71%
University of Arizona	77%	52%
University of California, Los Angeles	95%	79%
University of Florida	NR*	67%
University of Georgia	87%	63%
University of Illinois	92%	75%
University of Iowa	84%	62%
University of Maryland	87%	64%
University of Michigan	94%	82%
University of Minnesota	NR*	51%
University of North Carolina	94%	80%
University of Texas	88%	65%
University of Virginia	NR*	91%
University of Washington	91%	72%
University of Wisconsin	NR*	74%

NR* Institutions not reporting retention data.
Source: University of Kentucky, 2001

CONCLUSIONS REGARDING COLLEGE AND UNIVERSITY PREPARATION

The biggest question facing college and university presidents and state legislators is, where is the money coming from to pay for the increased salaries, the expansion of facilities, and the increased maintenance costs that would result from a dramatic increase in enrollment? College administrations are having a difficult time with increased health costs, keeping salaries competitive, and the increased cost of just keeping the doors open without a dramatic new increase. What's more, they can barely deal with the complications of providing a good college education for minorities, immigrants, and students with disabilities with their current staff and budget. State legislatures are cutting budgets, not expanding them. State budgets are becoming tighter, not looser.

The result of the "college for everyone" philosophy would result in colleges and universities having to compromise their mission statements. They would become less institutions of research and professional training and more and more like glorified community colleges. They would have such great demands due to increased undergraduate enrollments that they would have to sacrifice graduate programs. Even if they could shift millions of students to local community colleges, who would in turn sacrifice all vocational training programs, the demand for upper-division course offerings would multiply to the extent that something would have to give. Colleges and universities would no longer retain their place as the home and birthplace of new thinking and innovation and would instead become training grounds for technocrats.

7

WHAT EMPLOYERS EXPECT

Just as colleges and universities have certain expectations for future students, employers too have a right to expect certain job qualifications of their future employees. Some of the simple qualifications employers usually cite include expecting employees to get to work on time, expecting regular attendance, getting along with others, and having the ability to learn on the job. These are the bare minimum. Some employers want their employees to have the ability to read, write, spell, and do simple arithmetic. It is rare for an employer to ask that future employees have a basic knowledge of algebra, have knowledge of the humanities, or understand the basic principles of physics. Many employers ask that their future employees know how to use a computer keyboard and perhaps a simple word processing system such as Microsoft Word or Word Perfect. Some may even want their employees to know how to construct spreadsheets using software like Excel or other programs. The ability to learn quickly ("on-the-job training") is still the major job requirement for most employers.

Quotations from several employer groups point out their different expectations.

"In addition to job performance skills, and interpersonal skills, young people preparing for jobs in an economy of high technology must have a good working knowledge of computers to be able to be productive in most occupational areas" (South Carolina Council of Vocational Education 1990, pp. 6–7).

"What I want in a new worker, no high school can supply—a twenty-six year-old with three previous employers. Young people lack discipline; they expect to be catered to; they don't want to do the dirty jobs; they don't respect authority . . . they are neither numerate nor literate; they can't make change; they don't understand the importance of customer service" (Zemsky 1994, p. 4).

A study by G. C. Petty (Petty et al. 1990) at the University of Tennessee indicated that 80.5 percent of the employers surveyed in their 1990 study indicated that secondary vocational graduates had better entry-level work skills than recent high school graduates without vocational education. A study by McNelley and others (1991) showed that "small and large-sized firms valued secondary vocational–technical programs as a source for finding entry-level employees above other sources. The majority of these firms valued a high school diploma over other types of listed educational background" (McNelley et al. 1991, p. 19).

T. Bailey in the *Educational Researcher Journal* indicated that his survey of employers revealed "the secondary school system in the United States is too oriented toward college, thereby neglecting the majority of students who will never receive a baccalaureate degree" (Bailey 1993, p. 15).

The Business Needs Assessment Survey was administered by the Office of Institutional Research at Northern Virginia Community College and discovered that work ethics, communication abilities, the ability to learn on the job, motivation and initiative, and working with others were skills considered by the majority of employers to be "very important." Less than half the employers interviewed thought that skills such as special technical job skills or work experience were "very important." The overall survey indicated, "The new workplace requires adaptive and innovative workers with strong interpersonal skills. Emerging and existing workers will be expected to have as broad a set of skills as was previously required only of supervisors and management" (Gabriel et al. 2003, pp. 38–39).

In May 1992, twenty-five major employers in Canada stated that employers in that nation were looking for the following traits in future employees:

- People who can communicate, think, and continue to learn throughout their lives.

- People who can demonstrate positive attitudes and behaviors, responsibility, and adaptability.
- People who can work with others. (McLaughlin 1995)

Despite what employers say to the contrary, many educational policy makers still insist that a college education is required. There is little doubt a background in vocational education courses plus a willingness to work hard is what is preferred by many employers. There is still, however, an insistence that vocational education in "dumbing down" the curriculum.

DECLINE IN CONGRESSIONAL SUPPORT FOR NONCOLLEGE-BOUND STUDENTS

The U.S. Congress is currently busy undermining the original intent of Carl D. Perkins Vocational and Applied Technology Act by changing the name to "career and technical education." The name change is symbolic of efforts by academic elitists to replace vocational education and tech prep with college-oriented programs. Susan K. Sclafani, the Department of Education's assistant secretary of education, stated on June 9, 2004, "Everyone has to be a thinker—not just a pair of strong hands with a willingness to work. We're looking at this as a different entity. . . . All kids need a solid core in academics" (Cavanaugh 2004b, p. 30). There is something not only elitist but also actually demeaning toward people who like to work with their hands in this statement. Most citizens have no problem with a strong pair hands for an auto mechanic, a plumber, a carpenter, a nurse, or even a physician. Let us take a look at recent statistics by the Bureau of Labor Statistics related to the fifty jobs that are going to be needed in the next ten years and what kind of training employers expect.

Table 7.1 provides a realistic look at where the jobs are today for noncollege graduates and what type of preparation employers expect. It also indicates that short- to long-term on-the-job training is all that is necessary for most of the jobs listed. It is certainly true that there are a great many high-tech jobs needed in the future that require a college education. We need college professionals. We also need skilled workers. Secondary schools traditionally helped prepare students for the world of work. Many of those previously

Table 7.1. Jobs of the Future for Noncollege Graduates and Their Requirements

Job Description	Employer Needs 2002	Employer Needs Projected 2012	Percent Change	Training Necessary (On-the-Job Training—OJT)
Medical Assistants	364,600	579,400	59%	Moderate OJT
Social and Human Services	305,200	453,900	49%	Moderate OJT
Home Health Aides	579,700	858,700	48%	Short-term OJT
Dental Assistants	266,000	379,000	42%	Moderate OJT
Personal and Home Care	607,600	853,500	40%	Short-term OJT
Security Guards	995,500	1,312,600	32%	Short-term OJT
Receptionists	1,100,300	1,424,900	30%	Short-term OJT
Counter and Retail Clerks	435,800	550,200	26%	Short-term OJT
Nursing Aides	1,375,300	1,718,100	25%	Short-term OJT
Police and Sheriffs	618,800	771,600	25%	Long-term OJT
Bill and Account Collectors	413,000	513,900	24%	Short-term OJT
Customer Service Representatives	1,894,100	2,353,800	24%	Short-term OJT
Correctional Officers	427,100	530,500	24%	Moderate OJT
Electricians	659,400	813,900	23%	Long-term OJT
Truck Drivers, Light Delivery	1,022,200	1,259,200	23%	Short-term OJT
Truck Drivers, Heavy Delivery	1,767,100	2,103,700	19%	Moderate OJT
Industrial Truck and Tractor Operators	593,700	659,500	11%	Short-term OJT
Teacher Assistants	1,276,700	1,579,800	23%	Short-term OJT
Combined Food Preparation and Serving Workers	1,989,600	2,443,900	23%	Short-term OJT
Landscaping and Groundskeeping	1,074,400	1,311,000	22%	Short-term OJT
Packaging and Filling Machine Operator	86,600	468,300	21%	Short-term OJT
Firefighters	281,900	340,400	21%	Long-term OJT
Sales Representatives	1,857,100	2,213,400	19%	Moderate OJT
Plumbers, Pipe Fitters, and Steam Fitters	492,100	584,100	19%	Long-term OJT
Telecommunications Line Installers and Representatives	167,400	198,800	19%	Long-term OJT
Janitors and Cleaners	2,266,700	2,680,500	18%	Short-term OJT
Waiters and Waitresses	2,096,900	2,464,300	18%	Short-term OJT
Welders, Cutters, and Brazers	390,500	456,700	17%	Long-term OJT
Bus Drivers, School	452,500	528,300	17%	Short-term OJT
Maintenance and Repair Workers	1,265,600	1,472,400	16%	Moderate OJT

Table 7.1. (*continued*)

Job Description	Employer Needs 2002	Employer Needs Projected 2012	Percent Change	Training Necessary (On-the-Job Training—OJT)
Hosts and Hostesses	297,600	346,500	16%	Short-term OJT
Flight Attendants	104,000	120,600	16%	Long-term OJT
Bus Drivers, Intercity	201,900	232,500	15%	Moderate OJT
Cooks, Restaurant	727,100	842,800	16%	Long-term OJT
Chefs and Head Cooks	131,900	152,800	16%	Work experience
Cooks, Fast Food	588,100	617,200	5%	Short-term OJT
First-Line Supervisors Food Preparation	692,300	799,700	16%	Work experience
Retail Salespersons	4,075,800	4,671,700	15%	Short-term OJT
Supervisors, Retail Sales	1,798,100	1,961,500	9%	Work experience
Packers and Packagers	919,900	1,052,400	14%	Short-term OJT
Construction Laborers	937,800	1,070,500	14%	Short-term OJT
Construction Supervisors	633,000	722,000	14%	Work experience
Cashiers	3,431,700	3,885,800	13%	Short-term OJT
Child Care Workers	1,352,700	1,352,700	12%	Short-term OJT
Painters	447,600	499,600	12%	Moderate OJT
General Office Clerks	2,991,100	3,300,700	10%	Short-term OJT
Carpenters	1,208,600	1,331,000	10%	Long-term OJT
Tellers	530,400	580,200	9%	Short-term OJT
Maids and Housekeepers	1,492,100	1,628,700	9%	Short-term OJT
Executive Secretaries and Administrative Assistants	1,526,300	1,658,500	9%	Moderate OJT

Source: Bureau of Labor Statistics, U.S. Department of Labor, 2004.

wonderful presecretarial training programs, drafting programs, metal and woodworking programs, and preschool training programs for young children are now gone and have been replaced by programs that emphasize academic course work. This is a tragedy and ignores at least a third of our students, who traditionally benefited from vocational programs in high schools. Gone, too, are many of the school-to-work programs. Tech preparation has become another program for the academically talented. Gone are vocational counselors in many school districts. Gone are job fairs. Although regional occupation programs (ROPs) are still available in many, if not most, school districts, the counseling of students into those programs is often haphazard and a way for students to earn credits rather than real job training. It does not take a rocket scientist to look at the fifty jobs listed above and come to the conclusion that high schools can be a great help in preparing students to fill the needs of the

coming job market. It also does not take a rocket scientist to come to the conclusion that if high schools do not help fill that need, immigrants will be coming across the borders in all directions because there are jobs available and employers need workers. The American business community will fill those jobs
one way or another. It is quite possible that because of the refusal of education
policy makers to return vocational training to its proper place in schools, millions of young people will be forced onto welfare and the unemployment rolls
because they are not prepared for the future. The jobs that should be going to
our own young citizens will be going to immigrant workers.

8

CONCLUSION

There is a conspiracy going on that is based on making students feel guilty if they do not go on to college. That conspiracy is not only unfair, it is not healthy to the values and needs of our nation. We need to value people for the jobs they do and be proud of their willingness to be part of the system. There is absolutely nothing wrong with being a letter carrier, a gas station attendant, a grocery checker, a waitress, a truck driver, or a secretary. These are important jobs to our nation as well as to our way of life. It may be true that people who do not go to college do not make as much money, but money does not always mean happiness. Many people who are letter carriers, gas station attendants, or grocery checkers are often very happy with both themselves and their jobs. There is no need to make them feel unsuccessful or guilty.

Success is a relative thing; who is to say that someone who is doing a job in a position that he or she likes, even if it does not make a great deal of money, is not a success? The economy of our nation will not come crumbling down because half the population does not have the interest or perhaps the verbal or mathematical ability to go on to college. There are also many entrepreneurs, professional athletes, and musicians who did not go on to college who make millions of dollars a year. Likewise, we should not assume that all workers who do go on to college make a great deal of money. Many college graduates take jobs as teachers, social workers, and attorneys that do not pay high salaries. They, too, may like the jobs they do and are not necessarily motivated by a large income.

LIFELONG LEARNING

Studies indicate that the average adult uses the educational system as a tool for vocational preparation, personal growth, or recreational learning. The educational system includes adult schools, ESL classes, special computer software classes, sales product update classes, university extension programs, licensing or credential requirement classes, senior craft programs, and university classes for working adults. Schooling is not simply something young people participate in while they are young. Education for adults today is a lifelong endeavor. We choose education as we need or want it, regardless of age. People may go for long periods without taking any course work or specialized training but specialized learning may take place in churches, synagogues, mosques, adult schools, senior centers, neighborhood schools, or via the Internet. The educational course work of the future may not be formal but is nevertheless structured learning with lessons to be learned and some type of evaluation to determine if the tasks were completed. This is particularly the case for technical skill training that is currently conducted by many employers for their employees. Employees who do not continue their skill development will soon become obsolete—and the first to be let go in hard times.

Education for Americans has become a continuum where adults enter and exit the education stream at different points in their lives. The traditional concept of colleges—where students attend after high school and finish four years later—is not true anymore. People now take classes all their lives. This will continue to be the case in the future.

SPECIFIC RECOMMENDATIONS

We need to:

- Compare what the student can do and not force him or her into some type of "cookie cutter" or one-size-fits-all program.

- Identify student talents and interests while they are still in middle school. Capitalize on those talents when counseling them into high school programs that fit their abilities.
- Utilize Howard Gardner's multiple intelligences approach to vocational preparation.
- Reinstate vocational education programs in high schools that are relevant to today's jobs.
- Refocus tech prep and Carl Perkins grants so that they do not favor the academically talented students over students who are good with their hands but not interested or talented in academics.
- Expand ROP course offerings but be certain they are truly job preparation programs and not just places for students to earn credits.
- Publicize job opportunities that do not require a college education.
- Provide smaller schools with more individual attention for all students.
- Find ways to fully fund education.
- Make every attempt possible to alleviate child poverty and its causes in the United States.
- Extend the high school program to include after-school, Saturday, and evening programs. Make those programs available to adults.
- Provide a closer link between high schools and community colleges.
- Be certain that community colleges are not used to handle the overflow of universities at the expense of vocational programs.
- Create Adopt-a-School programs to provide tutors, equipment, and financial support for schools.
- Create a closer link between labor unions and vocational education.
- Promote apprenticeship programs and job shadowing where possible.
- Take the politics out of education. Education should never be used to promote a particular agenda.
- Build new and better schools. School climate is handicapped by worn-out buildings.
- Recruit vocational teachers from industry to ensure that job training is current.
- Find other means of evaluation rather than standardized tests to evaluate student progress. Do not punish teachers and administrators who work in areas where poverty and parent illiteracy are high.

- Provide vocational training programs for identified special education students. Begin those programs early in their high school career.

LOOKING FORWARD

College in the future will become a different kind of place. While traditional colleges will maintain their role as research institutions, much of professional training may be accomplished by satellite campuses or specialized schools for adults who work full time. The University of Phoenix is just such a plan, but there are many other similar types of programs emerging in every state. The average age of a college graduate is twenty-eight, but the average age of students completing a bachelor's degree at the University of Phoenix is thirty-seven years of age. The number of adults taking course work at Elder Hostel in the past five years was 546,000. The number of adults participating in work-related or ESL adult education courses was at the highest level ever. Adults will increasingly jump on and off the education network as their needs and interests dictate. There are many types of education in this nation. Academic learning is only one kind.

Let us hope our colleges and universities continue to succeed in their excellent efforts in research and other fields that demand a rigorous full-time devotion to a discipline over a long period of time. Let us continue to fund and encourage educational programs of all types that meet the demands of technology in a competitive economic world. Let us continue to support our public schools, for they are one of our greatest contributions to democracy and civilization. Let us *not* support programs that are sponsored by elitist mentalities and that ignore the realities of our schools and universities. College really isn't for everyone—but a life full of happiness, success, and fulfillment is. Let us keep our perspective and focus.

REFERENCES

Abbott, R. D., K. G. Hill, R. F. Catalano, and D. Hawkins. 2000. "Predictions of Early High School Dropout: A Test of Five Theories," *Journal of Educational Psychology 92*(3): 568–82.

American Federation of Teachers Press Release. 2004. "New Bush FY 2005 Budget for No Child Left Behind Comes Up Short." January 12. Available at www.aft.org/press/2004.

Amrein, S., and J. Berliner. 2002. "Impact of High Stakes Testing on Student Academic Performance," *Education Policy Research Unit* (Tempe, Arizona).

Bailey, T. 1993. "Can Youth Apprenticeships Thrive in the United States?" *Educational Researcher Journal 22*(3): 11–16.

Baily, Martin N., and Solow, Robert M. (Summer 2001). "International Productivity Comparisons Built from the Firm Level," *The Journal of Economic Perspectives 15*(3): 151–72.

Berkner, H., and J. Cataldi. 2002. *Descriptive Summary of 1995–1996 Beginning Postsecondary Students: Six Years Later.* Washington, D.C.: U.S. Department of Education, National Center for Education Statistics.

Bureau of Labor Statistics. 2004. *Outcome Goal 1.2: Increase the Number of Youth Making a Successful Transition to Work.* U.S. Department of Labor Annual Report, Fiscal Year 2003. Washington, D.C.: U.S. Department of Labor.

Bureau of Labor Statistics, Office of Employment Projections. 2004. *Fastest Growing Occupations Requiring Work Experience or On-the Job Training*. Washington D.C.: U.S. Department of Labor.

Campbell, L. 2003–2004. "Strong as the Weakest Link: Urban High School Dropouts," *High School Journal* 87(2) (December–January): 16–23.

Cavanaugh, S. 2004a. "Tougher Exam for GED Spurs Ups and Downs," *Education Week* (July 28): 9.

———. 2004b. "Bush Plan Calls for More Rigor in Vocational Education," *Education Week* (June 9): 9.

Chen, E., and E. Hayasaki. 2004. "Bush Links More Rigorous Schooling to Getting Jobs," *Los Angeles Times*, April 7.

College Board Examinations. 2004a. *The New SAT: Algebra and Functions*. Princeton, N.J., www.collegeboard.com/newsat/hs/curriculum.html.

College Board Examinations. 2004b. *The New SAT and Your School System*. Princeton, N.J., www.collegeboard.com/newsat/hs/curriculum.html.

Committee on Education and the Workforce. 2004. "Greenspan: Raising Education Standards, Training Workers Key to Creating American Jobs," *Los Angeles Times*, (March 11): 18.

Crosse, S., M. Burr, D. Cantor, C. A. Hagen, and I. Hantman. 2001. "Wide Scope, Questionable Quality: Drug and Violence Prevention Efforts in American Schools." *Report on the Study on School Violence and Prevention*. Washington, D.C.: U.S. Department of Education, Planning and Evaluation Service.

Devlin, K. 2000. *The Math Gene*. London: Basic Books.

Forgione, P. D. 1998. "Achievement in the United States: Progress since *A Nation At Risk*?" Remarks delivered before the Center for Education Reform and Empower America, April 13, New York.

Futrell, H., and I. Rotberg. 2002. "Predictable Casualties: High Stakes Standardized Tests Equal Higher Dropout Rates," *Education Week* (October 2): 17.

Gabriel, G. 2002. *Employee Characteristics and Skills Valued by Northern Virginia Employers*. Annandale: Northern Virginia Community College, Office of Institutional Research.

Gabriel, G., et al. 2003. "Employee Characteristics and Skills Valued by Northern Virginia Employees," *Business Needs Assessment Survey*. Annandale: Northern Virginia Community College.

Gardner, H. 1983. *Frames of Mind: The Theory of Multiple Intelligences*. New York: Basic Books.

———. 2000. *Intelligence Reframed: Multiple Intelligences for the 21st Century*. New York: Basic Books.

Gayler, K., N. Chudowski, M. Hamilton, N. Kafer, and N. Yeager. 2004. *State High School Exit Exams: A Maturing Reform.* Washington, D.C.: Center for Education Policy.

Gayler, K., N. Chudowski, N. Kober, and M. Hamilton, M. 2003. *The Growing Influence of Exit Exams.* Washington, D.C.: Center for Education Policy.

Gerstner, L. V., R. D. Semerad, D. P. Doyle, and W. Johnston. 1994. *Reinventing Education.* New York: Dutton, 1994.

Greene, J. P., and M. A. Winter. 2004. "Pushed Out or Pulled Up? Exit Exams and Dropout Rates in Public High Schools," *Manhattan Institute for Policy Research,* no. 5 (May): 39.

Halperin, S. 1998. "The Forgotten Half Revisited: American Youth and Young Families, 1988–2008." American Youth Policy Forum, January, Washington, D.C.

Haney, W., G. Madaus, L. Abrams, A. Wheelock, J. Mao, and I. Gruin. 2004. *The Education Pipeline in the United States, 1970–2000.* Boston: National Board of Education Testing and Public Policy.

Harris D., M. Handel, and L. Mishel. 2004. "Education and the Economy Revisited: How Schools Matter," *Peabody Journal of Education* 79(1): 36–63.

Hodgkinson, H. L. 2003. "Leaving Too Many Children Behind." *Institute for Educational Leadership,* April, Washington, D.C. Available at www.iel.org.

Holland, R. 2003. "High School Crisis: 3 in 10 Drop Out." *School Reform News* (January 1): 36–37.

International Labor Organization. 2003. *Key Indicators of the Labor Market 2001–2002.* New York: United Nations Publication, 92-2.

Jennings, J., and D. Rentner. 2002. *High Schools That Work.* Washington, D.C.: Center for Education Policy.

Keller, B. 2004. "Wisconsin Review Invites 'No Child Lawsuit,'" *Education Week* (May 26): 5.

Langer, S. K. 1973. *Philosophy in a New Key.* Cambridge, Mass.: Harvard University Press.

McLaughlin, M. 1995. *Employability Skills Profile: What Are Employers Looking For?* Greensboro, N.C. ERIC identifier: ED39.

McNelley, D. E., et al. 1991. *A Statewide Needs Assessment in Tennessee: Employers.* Knoxville: Department of Technical and Adult Education, University of Tennessee.

Meeder, H. 2003. *Policy Directions for Career and Technical Education: Office of Vocational and Adult Education.* Washington, D.C.: U.S. Department of Education.

Morest, V. S. 2004. *The Academic Mission of Community Colleges: Structural Responses to the Expansion of Higher Education.* Paper prepared for the annual meeting of the American Research Association, San Diego, Calif.

National Center for Education Statistics. 1997. *Education and the Economy: An Industry Report*. Washington D.C.: U.S. Department of Education, Office of Educational Research and Improvement, 3–4.

———. 1999. *Dropout Rates in the United States: 1998*. Washington, D.C.: U.S. Department of Education, Office of Educational Research and Evaluation.

———. 2000a. *Coming of Age in the 1990s: The Eighth Grade Class of 1988 12 Years Later*. Washington, D.C.: U.S. Department of Education, Office of Educational Research and Improvement.

———. 2000b. *Undergraduate Diversity, National Postsecondary Student Aid Study, 1999-2000*. Washington, D.C.: U.S. Department of Education.

———. 2000c. *Vocational Education in the United States: Toward the Year 2000*. Washington, D.C.: U.S. Department of Education.

———. 2002a. *Community College Academic Preparation, and Outcomes*. Washington, D.C.: U.S. Department of Education.

———. 2002b. *Descriptive Summary of 1995–1996 Beginning Postsecondary Students: Six Years Later*. Washington, D.C.: U.S. Department of Education.

———. 2002c. *Twelfth Graders Show Declining Interest and Effort in School*. Washington, D.C.: U.S. Department of Education.

———. 2003. *The Condition of Education*. Washington, D.C.: U.S. Department of Education.

———. 2004a. *The High School Transcript Study: A Decade of Change in Curriculum and Achievement, 1990-2000*. Washington, D.C.: U.S. Department of Education.

———. 2004b. *Public High School Dropouts and Completers from the Common Core of Data for School Year 2000-2001*. Washington, D.C.: U.S. Department of Education, Office of Educational Research and Improvement.

———. 2004c. *Student Effort and Educational Progress: The Condition of Education, 2004*. Washington, D.C.: U.S. Department of Education.

National Commission on Excellence in Education. 1983. *A Nation at Risk: The Imperative for Educational Reform*. Washington, D.C.: U.S. Government Printing Office.

Newman, J. 1992. *Twelfth Grade High School Interest in School*. Washington, D.C.: National Commission on Excellence in Education.

Office of Assessment and Institutional Data. 2002. *Benchmark Institutions and Retention Rates*. University of Kentucky, January.

Olson, L. 2004a. "Critics Float 'No Child' Revisions," *Education Week* (August 11): 16.

———. 2004b. "Government Offers Guidance on Standards and Testing," *Education Week* (May 26): 6.

——. 2004c. "No Child Left Behind Act Changes Weighed," *Education Week* (September 22): 23.

Petty, G. C., et al. 1990. Employer Ratings of Vocational Education Graduate Effectiveness. *A Research Study Exploring Business and Industry Employers Perceptions of Effectiveness of the Secondary Vocational Education Programs in Tennessee.* Nashville: University of Tennessee.

Piaget, J., and B. Inhelder. 1958. *The Growth of Logical Thinking.* New York: Basic Books.

Popham, J. W. 2004. "Shaping Up the 'No Child 'Act, Is Edge-Softening Really Enough?" *Education Week* (May 26): 34, 39.

Rainwater, R., and M. Smeeding. 1995. "Doing Poorly: The Real Income of American Children in a Comparative Perspective." Working Paper no. 127, *Luxembourg Income Study, Maxwell Study of Citizenship and Public Affairs.* Syracuse, N.Y.: Syracuse University.

Richardson, W. C. 2002. "A Peacetime Mission for Higher Education." Speech to the W. K. Kellogg Foundation, May, Minneapolis, Minnesota.

South Carolina Council of Vocational Education. Business and Industry Forum. 1990. *Vocational Technical Education*, Columbia, South Carolina.

Swanson, C. 2004. "The New Math on Graduation Rates," *Education Week* (July 28): 4.

University of California. 2004. "About the University of California's Mission." *University of California.* Available at www.universityofcalifornia.edu/aboutuc/.

University of Kentucky. 2001. *Retention and Graduation Rates.* Lexington, KY: Institution Research Reports, University of Kentucky, Lexington Campus.

University of Michigan. 2002. *Monitoring the Future 12th Grade Study: 1983, 1990, 1995 and 2000.* Ann Arbor: University of Michigan, Institute of Social Research.

University of Texas. 2004. "Mission Statement of the University of Texas." *University of Texas.* Available at www.utsystem.edu/mission.htm.

University of Wisconsin. 2004. "Mission Statement, Chancellor's Page." *University of Wisconsin.* Available at www.chancellor.wisc.edu/mission.html.

U.S. Department of Commerce, Bureau of the Census. 2002. *March Current Population Surveys, 1971–2001, Student Effort and Educational Progress.* Washington. D.C.: U.S. Department of Commerce, Bureau of the Census.

U.S. Department of Education, National Center for Education Statistics. 2000. *Dropout Rates in the United States: 1998*, NCES 2000-022, by Phillip Kaufman, Jin Y. Kwon, and Steve Kleain, Project Officer: Christopher D. Chapman. Washington D.C.: U.S. Department of Education.

U.S. Department of Education, National Center for Education Statistics. 2003. *The Condition of Education 2003*, NCES 2003-067. Washington D.C.: U.S. Department of Education.

U.S. Department of Education, Office of Education and Inprovement. March 1994. Reaching the Goals: Goal 2/High School Completion. Washington, D.C.: U.S. Department of Education.

U.S. Department of Education, Office of Special Education. 2003. *Date Analysis System, (DANS) Number of Children Ages 12–17 Served under IDEA, Part B by Disability*. Washington, D.C.: U.S. Department of Education, July 31.

U.S. Department of Labor, Bureau of Labor Statistics. 1989. *Handbook of Labor Statistics*. Washington, D.C.: U.S. Government Printing Office.

———. 1992. *Labor Composition and U.S. Productivity Growth, 1948–1990*. Bulletin 2426. Washington, D.C.: U.S. Department of Labor.

———. 1995. *Monthly Labor Review* 18, no. 8 (August): 175.

———. 2001. *Occupational Outlook Handbook*. Bulletin 2520. Washington, D.C.: U.S. Department of Labor.

Vives, O. 2001. "Latina Girls' High School Dropout Rate Highest in U.S." *National Organization for Women*, Fall. Available at www.now.org/nnt/fall-2001/latina.

William T. Grant Foundation. 1988a. *The Forgotten Half: Non-College Youth in America*. New York: Commission on Work, Family and Citizenship.

———. 1988b. *The Forgotten Half: Pathway to Success for America's Youth and Young Families*. New York: Commission on Work, Family and Citizenship.

World Almanac and Book of Facts. 2005. New York: World Almanac Books.

Zemsky, R. 1994. *What Employers Want: Employer Perspectives on Youth, the Youth Labor Market, and Prospects for a National System of Youth Apprenticeships*. Philadelphia, Penn.: National Center on the Educational Equality of the Workforce.

INDEX

ABOUT THE AUTHOR

Louis Rosen has worked as a teacher, counselor, and high school principal. After taking early retirement from the public schools, he administered various federal grants for the Center for Civic Education. The grants dealt with substance abuse and violence prevention programs primarily in secondary schools throughout the United States. He conducted teacher and administrator training programs in twenty-two states and the District of Columbia. The training was in inner-city, suburban, and rural school districts and included private schools, Indian reservation schools, and public schools. His impressions of the quality of schools, teachers, and administrators are based upon visits to classrooms, schools, and areas throughout the United States over the past fifteen years. His experience in visiting schools throughout the United States is unique.

Rosen has a bachelor's degree in history from U.C.L.A., a master of arts from California State University, Los Angeles, and a doctorate of philosophy degree from Claremont Graduate University. His book, *School Discipline Practices: Best Practices for School Administrators*, is used by school administrators throughout the United States as well as in college and university classes in school administration. He is married, has three children and five grandchildren, and resides in Pacific Palisades, California.